Harold Martin remembers

A Place in the Mountains

Harold Martin remembers A Place in the Mountains

Illustrated by Bill Drath

Peachtree Publishers, Ltd.

Selections from *A Place in the Mountains* narrated by the author are available on cassette tapes.

Published by
PEACHTREE PUBLISHERS, LTD.
494 Armour Circle, N.E., Atlanta, Georgia 30324

Copyright © 1979 Harold H. Martin, Text
      Wilfred H. Drath, Illustrations

Manufactured in the United States of America

First Edition—October 1979
Second Printing—February 1980

Library of Congress Cataloging in Publication Data

Martin, Harold H
 A place in the mountains.

 1. Mountain life—Georgia. 2. Georgia—Description and travel—1951-
3. Martin, Harold H. 4. Journalists—Georgia—Atlanta—Biography.
5. Atlanta—Biography. I. Title.
F291.2.M37 975.8'0094'3 79-67094
ISBN 0-931498-03-7

BHB

With grateful thanks to Mama, who found the house in the mountains, and filled it with love, and the joyful noises that dogs and children make, both ours and everybody's.

Contents

CONTENTS

Foreword

Many times in the years since I gave up the easygoing life of a newspaper columnist for the sterner regimen of a journalist-turned-historian-and-biographer, people who remembered the old columns about the mountains, and the cats and dogs, and birds and children, and chipmunks and travel and other trivia, have written me or stopped me on the street to ask if I had any plans to put these old essays in a book.

And of course, I *had* thought of it at random moments. Sometimes at home I'd even go upstairs on rainy days and burrow into the great stack of scrapbooks tucked away in a closet. And I'd sit there for an hour or more—back in spirit at the mountain place, or in Hawaii, or Hong Kong, or Rio, or in a foxhole in Korea or wherever. And the idle thought would float through my mind that someday these pieces might be organized into a book. But that was as far as it went. Just thinking.

Until about two years ago. Then one evening a young lady named Lee Schaffer came up to me at a party and we stood talking. Her husband, Bill, was teaching at Georgia Tech, she said, and her small son, Sammy, was in nursery school. She spoke with delight of my old columns on fathers and sons, squirrels and birds. And she thought other people might like them, too.

The thought came to both of us at once—why couldn't she go

through the old columns and organize them? And this she did, for a year or more, poring over the crumbly old scrapbooks.

Then all at once things started to fall into place. One day I was working at the Historical Society when a new book came in. It was published by a brand-new little company called Peachtree Publishers Limited. The title was *If I Found a Wistful Unicorn*, and it was written by Ann Ashford, and illustrated by Bill Drath. And because I thought it was a job well done, I sat down and wrote a note to Peachtree Publishers and told them so.

Not long afterward I got a phone call from Helen Elliott, the gentle lady behind Peachtree Publishers, asking if I would do something for her new and burgeoning little publishing house.

And that's how this book came about. It is the story of the place in the mountains and the people I knew and loved there, and to whom I always came home from wherever I might be wandering in days gone by. Reading the old essays over brings back to me a flood of memories. If they bring pleasure to those who read them in The *Atlanta Constitution*, and to younger readers, too, perhaps other books could follow—about people and places, pets and children and their strange ways, and about the men I knew and wrote about as they fought in three wars. Out of the musty scrapbooks a once-familiar cast of characters would emerge: Old Shim, and Sir Galahad, and Mrs. Unfriendly and Miss Twinkle, and the Queen of Love and Beauty, and Miss Eva, and old Knottyhaid, and Captain Midnight, the tomcat who wore my wristwatch to a back-fence fight . . . but that, if ever, is a project for the future.

Right now I am grateful to all those who helped me put this book together. And especially am I glad that whenever my words may have failed, the beautiful watercolors and the bright line drawings by Bill Drath have caught the mood and mystique of *A Place in the Mountains* that has been to me and so many others such a very special place.

Harold Martin
May 31, 1979

The Way It All Began

"Listen," I said, after she had talked about half an hour. "We can't afford a place in the mountains. Places in the mountains . . . ."

She sighed patiently. "That's what I've been trying to tell you," she said. "We can't afford *not* to have a place in the mountains. You know how expensive camps are, and with two children already camp age and two more who will be soon, just think how expensive it will be. Now with this little place, small as it is, we can just take them up there and turn them loose and it will be much less expensive. Why, in just two or three years we'll save much more than it costs."

"Wellllll," I said, remembering last year's camp bills and beginning to weaken a little. She has a sharp eye for changes in mood. She always knows when I am beginning to weaken. Sometimes she knows it before I do. She moved swiftly to the attack again.

"And another thing," she said, "you are always complaining that you cannot write at home. Up there, where everything is

quiet, we can fix you a little place where you can be all by yourself. Then you can sit down and write all you want to. Maybe you
can even get started on a book."

I pondered over this. I visualized myself sitting at the typewriter, looking off into sylvan solitudes, puffing a pipe reflec-
tively, like the pictures of authors you see in literary magazines. It
was a warming picture.

"O.K., O.K.," I said, giving up the struggle. So that's how I
came to have a place in the mountains. At least, that's how the
bank came to have a place in the mountains. But they are nice
people down at the bank. They let me carry the key.

It's a nice little place. I'll bet two people would be just as snug
as a bug in a rug in it. Six people are going to find it a little snug-
ger than that. But she was very proud of it.

"This," she said, flinging open the front door, and frightening a
family of chipmunks who were asleep on the sofa, "is the living
room. See the nice big stone fireplace. It will be cool enough to
have a fire every night, almost. It's 2,800 feet above sea level. Or
maybe 2,300, I forget which the man said."

"Fine," I said. "It's got a nice view across the valley. I can set
up my typewriter in here and write furiously."

"Oh, no," she said. "Not in here. This is going to be our bedroom. We'll build in bunks right here alongside the fireplace on
each side. Won't that be cozy?"

"It'll be too cozy." I said. "If I go a day without shaving, my
whiskers will catch on fire while I sleep."

I opened a door. "This is a nice big closet," I said, "maybe I
could set up in here to do my writing. I just need enough room
for a desk and a chair, and it has a window . . . ."

"Don't be silly," she said. "That's the bedroom. That's where
the girls will sleep."

"Not if they breathe deeply while they sleep," I said. "They'll
bump each other." I opened another door. It had a table and
some chairs in it. It had a window and about a mile away you
could see a corner of the lake, about the size of a handkerchief.

"Ah," I said. "Here's room . . . ."

3

"That," she said, "is the dining room. Except we aren't going to use it for a dining room. We'll eat on the back porch. This is going to be the boys' room. We'll put double-decker bunks in it."

We looked at the kitchen. It was a nice kitchen. You could stand in the middle of it and reach everything—the stove, the refrigerator, the pantry, the sink. But there was no room for a typewriter in it. If it had a typewriter in it, you couldn't reach anything. There wouldn't be anywhere to reach from, unless you went outside and reached through the window.

The back porch was nice, too, if you didn't want to swing a cat. There wasn't room enough to swing a cat. The bathroom was on the same scale. That's all there was.

"Look," I said, after surveying my new domain. "You put up a great selling talk about having a place where I could write. Just where in this rambling mansion do you see any place where a man could write?"

She seemed nonplussed for a minute. Then her eyes lighted up. "Come with me," she said. She went out on the back porch.

"Look," she said. She pointed up in the woods. There was an edifice there, a relic of the early days when certain amenities, such as plumbing, had not yet been introduced to the mountains.

"Wonderful," she said. "We'll put a little window in the side next to the lake and I'll make you some nice curtains. We'll get started on it just as soon as you paint the house and fix the screens and scrape down the floors and sand them and wax them and paint over the living room furniture and spade up the yard and plant it in grass and move the woodpile around to the back and fix that little place where the roof leaks and . . . ."

"Wait a minute," I said. "Who is going to do all these things?"

"Why, you are," she said. "Who did you suppose?"

I went in the house and got my typewriter and brought it out and put it in the car.

"Where are you going with that?" she said.

"I'm taking it back home," I said, "to pawn it. I see right now I'll never be needing it up here."

But I didn't take it home . . . .

4

The Maker of the Storms

That old hill over there has been around here a long time, I guess, for it looks worn and round-shouldered, shaggy and old. Time was, I suppose, when it was a proud mountain, standing up high, with snow on its crest and on its shoulders great scraps of bare granite all broken and jagged. But the winds and rains, the snows and the sunshines of many a million of years have worked on it and worn it down until now there isn't much left. Just a great green mound, sloping gently up 500 feet or more below the little valley, covered with trees whose roots go down to grip the solid rock that lies so close beneath the covering of leaf and mold.

But it still pretty well runs things around here. It makes the rains, I think, and somewhere along its flanks the thunder and the lightning live, and to me it dominates everything around— the gentler slopes over which it broods, and the lake which lies at its foot. And I know it dominates me, for I sit for hours looking at it marveling at its many moods, its stirring, and its stillness.

On sunshiny days it almost seems to smile, and the bright light twinkles and shines on its green leaves, and all its great spreading flank is a tapestry of many lights and shadows. Even with the sun overhead, it seems to make the light more bright, to serve as a great reflector that holds the light and passes it down into the valley multiplied.

But it does not seem to want the world it dominates to live too long in sunshine. Every day or so—even on what begins as the fairest of days—it hauls off and makes a storm. It is interesting to watch it do this. First it gathers round its head little wisps of gray cloud, thin as pipe smoke, and they begin to drift and stream out in ribbons along the crest. Then a bustling wind begins to blow and you can see the trees beyond the slope begin to nod and sway and whisper, "Here it comes." And then the little wisps of gray dip down into the valley, and at the crest big black clouds begin to boil, and lightning lances through them. And from somewhere deep in the bowels of the mountain the thunder stirs and groans, and the lightning dances more madly at the top, and there is a strange feeling in the air, as of something about to burst.

Then comes the rain. It comes down the mountain in a gray blanket and the wind picks it up and whips it in fragments and tatters, and it drives across the valley with the speed of horses running and it beats against the little house. And the wind cries like a child lost in the dark, and the trees in the yard writhe and thresh in their agony.

And the thunder sounds like the roar of cannon and the lightnings dance with blue and yellow flame above the thunder, and in the house we huddle, hearing the roar and the crying, the crashing and the rumble.

Day dies in this dark tumult, and night comes on, black and fearful. And then suddenly all is quiet and the old mountain lies there, its passion spent. Slowly, one by one, the gentle stars begin to peep over its shoulder, at first like scattered little lights seen through the topmost trees, and then as thick as fireflies, until finally the shaggy crest wears a glittering crown of them. And from its slopes the whippoorwill begins to call, and in the dark shadows at its foot the deer walk, seeking the open glades. And the old hill lies in the starlight, dreaming its dreams of the million years that have gone since it was a great mountain, high and proud, and the millions that are still to come before it will lie, at last, level with the plain.

Where Time Stands Still

One thing you feel the moment you arrive here in the hills is the timeless quality of the place, the ageless sense of peace and quietness and unchanging time. Men alter the face of the valleys, fill them with houses and roads and stores and factories. But they leave the hills alone or make changes so trivial they leave but a little scar.

I know, for example, there are chicken houses on the slopes of that big hill that looms across the valley from my house. But I can't see them nor hear them. So as far as I am concerned they are not there.

The old dirt road that wound along the shoulder of the mountain is a wide paved highway now, but I can't see it either and the sound of the automobiles traveling on it is muted to a whisper by a million leaves on a thousand trees. Even the old groundhog who lives under the house and takes the sun in the open meadow is not disturbed by the busy road.

In a world that changes so fast that only the very young can adjust to it without strain, it's a comfort somehow to find a place that does not change. The look of the lake with the blue hills around it is just the same as it was fifteen years ago. The light lies the same on the water and the feel of the wind in the morning and the sound of it by night is just the same. And the sound of the crows calling far off and the sight of the hawk swooping lazy and slow are just as they always were.

Only the faces change. The folk who started this place up here long ago when they were young grow older and more gray, and between each summer and the next one or two move on to a happier and even more changeless land, leaving behind them warm memories of their kindness and their laughter. Babies come and metamorphose in the space of a handful of summers from little tadpoles, helpless and tender, into tall and muscular people or slim and beautiful people who fall in love and get married and have babies and bring them to snooze in baskets by the lakeside under the same old trees they were laid to sleep under when they were young.

And here begins a cycle of life that is itself unchanging, a movement from shade to sun and water and back again to shade. For by the sleeping babies the old folks sit on benches under the trees and out in the water the young folks romp and on the dock the young mothers and fathers snooze and gossip and soak up the sun. And each without thinking about it follows a cycle of life as unchanging as the seasons, from the baby basket to the water and the sun and back again at last to the old folks' benches under the trees.

The First Big Storm of Summer

The day was hot and still and dry and though the sun filtered palely through a veil of cloud, the old-timers said it didn't mean anything. There had been many of these overcast days, but no rain since April. The mountains were green with that lush rich green of the first leaf, but the dirt road around the lake was a river of dust, and the powdery dust lay thick on the trees beside the road.

Evening came, and with it an unnatural stillness. The little breeze, that usually comes with the setting sun, did not blow. There was a sense of waiting in the air, a close, smothering feeling of something about to burst or break or shatter. The birds sang fitfully. The bobwhite called a nervous note or two, then stopped. Then all at once, there was a great silence, as if nothing lived upon the earth. It was growing dark fast. Too dark, too fast, for the time of day.

The first great crash of thunder and glare of lightning was like the sudden blasting of a mighty cannon. It tore the sky apart and through the riven heavens the deluge fell. Sharp crack close by, and far-off rumble. Lightning in sheets and lightning in dancing spears stabbed from the black sky toward the drowning earth.

Boom and thunder, crackle, crash, and bang, for half an hour the cannonade continued. Under the bed the dog whimpered. On the beds the children, big-eyed and frightened, watched through the windows the great display of heavenly artillery. The lights went out, and in the dark the flicker of candles threw ghostly dancing shadows on the walls. Against the windows the wind-blown rain pelted like buckshot. The candles went out and had to be lighted again and again.

Suddenly all was quiet. The lightning ceased. The thunder no longer rolled. The rain died to a gentle patter on the roof. High in the sky, through the torn black clouds, a few bright stars appeared. Then, far down the valley, we heard the deep murmur, growing nearer and nearer.

Swiftly the sound grew and suddenly the wind was upon us. The old house seemed to brace itself against the push of the wind. It groaned deep in its joints as solid timbers took the strain. Outside, there was a moaning and a shrieking as tortured trees bent, their limbs writhing. I wondered how the deer were making out on the hillsides, how the birds which had sung so nervously were surviving, riding the leaping, tossing branches of the trees.

It lasted maybe fifteen minutes, this maniac wind. Then it was gone and the night was quiet except for the gentle murmur of the slow, steady rain.

The storm had gone, but it had left the house lifeless and dead. The stove, with supper half cooked, was cold. The electric hot water heater would not work. The lights no longer burned. The dead refrigerator, defrosting, dripped until all within it was a sodden mass.

There was nothing to do but go to bed and contemplate, morosely, on how dependent folks have become on all their gadgets. And how helpless they are when the lightning blazes and the big winds roar across the mountains.

Every Time of Day Is the Best Time

Somehow I think that mornings are the best time—the very early morning when the mist begins to lift from the valley and the birds begin to sing. That is the time you sit on the porch, watching the edge of the woods, hoping to see a deer.

Sometimes I think the early afternoon is the best time, when the valley is a bowl of golden light and there is no sound at all except the faint thin singing of the little insects that live in the deep grass of the meadow.

And then I think that late afternoon is the best, when the cool winds begin to blow, clearing the valley of its midday heat, and the clouds begin to pile up over the lake, and the sinking sun paints them pink, and then red and gold, and the surface of the lake is a ripple of gold.

But the best time, I guess, is a little later, when the first bright star comes out and hangs like a big silver-blue lamp up there all alone.

This is the time when the last bird song dies, and the frogs begin to talk back and forth from the reedy places where the little streams feed into the lake. Frogs are like families, they all talk at once, and pretty soon it's hard to make out one frog's voice from another. They are all going cherrunk, cherrunk, together.

Except once in a while they will all stop at once, and the night will be very still. Then one old frog will go ch-u n k, as if he's asking a question, and they'll all start up again together.

The whippoorwills are different, though. They carry on a polite conversation. Far up the valley one will call, then he'll wait a minute, and down the valley another will answer. And in the leafy woods back of the house another will come in. But they don't try to all talk at once, and one will wait till the other finishes his "Will" and makes that little cluck at the end before he starts his "whip."

After a while the frogs and the whippoorwills alike fall silent, and the tree frogs and the crickets take over, with their high thin singing.

Sitting there on the porch in the dark, watching the stars climb over the dark shape of the mountain, seeing the lights of the celestial cities shining far out in space, and listening to the sounds of the singing night, I sometimes feel a strange sense of having moved far back in time.

This is the way the night looked and sounded to the Indians 500 years ago—these same stars in the same patterns against the black night, these same frog sounds and bird sounds, and cricket sounds—coming down unchanged through all the ages.

Then a new star moves in the sky over the mountain, a red winking star, and a new sound comes, the deep beat of big engines. And the plane bound for Chicago passes over, pulling hard as it climbs, and the spell of the night is broken and it is time to sleep.

The Seasons Pass in Grand Review

It was a day that teased and tantalized from dawn to dusk, passing all the seasons in review, as if to show the one-day visitors the changing faces of mountain weather. It was, at times, as bland and gentle as April, as hot as burning summer, as crisp as autumn and, for one strange half-hour, as clammy-cold as deepest winter. But to everyone it brought some small and gracious gift.

For the bass fisherman, casting his lure along the brushy banks, there were the drifting tattered clouds which dappled the shallows with the pools of shadow where bass like to lie and feed, and brusque little thunder squalls, filled with icy rain, that filled the air with an electric tension and stirred the fish to action.

For the bream fisherman, anchored solidly over the deep waters, there were long hours of unbroken sun that fixed the mind in that pleasant torpor which a man must achieve before he can happily fish for bream—a kind of sun-struck hypnosis, in which the only sense left alive is the sense of touch, which responds when a fat bream hits the catawba worm and the feel of his frantic tugging comes up from the depths, like an electric shock, along the line and down the quivering pole and through the forearm into the innermost depths of the fisherman's soul.

For those who simmered slowly on the dock, drowsily turning

with the moving sun, there was the blessed but temporary relief of deep cold water to take the sting and bite from sunburned hide. For those who sought neither fish nor sun, but with the wisdom of years snoozed the day away in hammocks swung beneath the shade of trees, there was the blessing of an amiable little breeze that came and romped awhile and scampered away again like the casual visitation of a friendly puppy.

Of all the day's changing moods, though, the strangest came in the early afternoon to chase away the blistering midday heat. Suddenly there was no sun and the ghost of February walked the mountain. Cold fog rolled down the valley, shrouding lake and hill in a thick, white mist.

There was cold in the heart of the cloud, and folk who an hour before were grateful for a cooling breeze thought suddenly of oak logs burning on a hearth, and the good feel of wool against the skin. It was hard to believe that in July, in Georgia, there could be such cold.

And then the sun burned through, and the fog was gone, and summer lay upon the hills again, and a summer dusk came down and darkness like a black cat stole quietly in to set the frogs to chunking and the whippoorwill to crying.

That night, by the water, there were fireworks that filled the air with quick-dying stars of red and blue and yellow, and things that went "bang" to set the small boys whooping and the babies to crying.

Then everybody, nearly a hundred in all, lighted sparklers, and somebody started up the Star-Spangled Banner and the sound of the singing floated far over the water and over the hills, and the Fourth of July was over.

Mountain Storms Never Last Long

Another big thunderstorm is roaring and banging and crashing through the hills. There have been rains before, but nothing like this, for the great jagged streaks of lightning are darting at the mountain tops in yellow spears of flame and great white sheets of lightning are flashing in the valleys. The noise is tremendous, like a thousand giant cannon firing together—first the earsplitting crack of the lightning striking in the woods nearby and the dance of the flame on the power line running into the house. And then the booming, rumbling, grinding noise of the further thunder.

The little house seems isolated in the midst of all this flashing light and noise, rocking under the blows, leaking from a dozen cracks, with the rain blown in by the wind at the windows. It is a cold and icy rain from the highest sky and it falls in great wind-blown sheets, shutting off all sight of the surrounding hills. Sitting here, trying to write, is like sitting in a great metal cauldron on which somebody is banging with iron hammers.

The kids were at the table on the back porch, eating, when the first great thunderclap came out of a still sky and one, a visitor, leaped from her chair in terror.

"Who did that?" she yelled.

"God," said an older one calmly, munching his sandwich.

The dog suffers most when the big storms come. He runs from room to room, whining, and you can't hold him in your arms and comfort him. He struggles free and runs under a bed and then another big flash-bang comes and he scurries out and crouches in a corner. The only way to calm him is to catch him and put him on a bed and cover him with pillows and sit there with him, talking soothingly.

That's Mama's job. She's been through many of these things and she takes them in stride. She likes to sit on the porch, watching the big thunderheads pile up over the mountain. She stays there, exulting in the splendor and the power and the terror of the coming storm, until the cold rain begins to drive in on the porch and the lightning is dancing all around. Then she comes in and pulls all the switches, cutting off the current from the stove and the water heater, and turning off the lights. Then she puts candles around, red Christmas candles burning cheerily in the gloom and gathers the kids around and reads to them, or starts a game of charades until the flashing and the thunder are all gone.

They never last long, these mountain storms, for even nature cannot stay at this peak of rage for long. It is like a wild drunk, suddenly gone berserk, shouting and screaming and thrashing about, and suddenly, spent, falling quiet.

It is over now. The bellowing and flashing have ended. Far off in the hills the thunder dies to a growling mutter. The light comes back to the sky, and all that can be heard now is the slow and gentle sobbing of the dwindling rain.

An Old Mountain Custom — Feuding

In the manner of all good mountaineers, I am now engaged in a feud with my neighbor down the road, a gentleman of many virtues, but one who, in his attitude toward automobiles, still lives in the era of the long linen duster. By this I mean that he gazes upon his automobile as something which must be pampered and cajoled and nursed like a child. He is constantly worrying about his car, wondering whether or not it is breathing properly through its oil filter, whether the gasoline it is getting is giving it the proper nourishment, and whether or not there is enough pressure in the tires.

He is also always giving advice to other people about their automobiles, and is always trying to persuade me that the only way to drive the gravel road down the mountain is to travel at a speed of ten miles an hour. At this speed, he insists, if you hit a rock it does no damage to the fabric of the tires, whereas if you go roaring along at fifteen miles an hour, you blow big holes in your tires and never get where you are going. I point out to him that at a speed of ten miles an hour you never get where you are going, either, so what's the difference?

Brooding over my friend's automania, I decide it will be a fine idea to play a trick on him, thinking maybe that he will be cured

of his obsession. So I obtain from a fireworks establishment one of these devices which you attach to a man's car so that it will go off with a loud noise when he steps on the starter. I enlist the aid of a mechanically minded young man, who attaches this to my friend's automobile while he is sitting comfortably on my front porch, partaking of refreshment, and wait eagerly until it is time for him to go home so I can witness what happens when he steps on the starter.

Well, it is even better than I expected. He gets in the car and his wife gets in on the other side, and a noted Southern editor of my acquaintance starts climbing in the back seat and about this time my friend steps on the starter. First there is a medium-sized "Bang!", and black smoke starts boiling out from under the hood. This is followed by a loud shrieking, whistling sound, and I note that my friend is thrashing about in the front seat as if he is beset by yellowjackets. He is shouting hoarsely in wild alarm and is grabbing at every knob and handle on the dashboard, trying to shut off the engine, turn off the lights, throw the car out of gear and release the brakes. He is in quite a frenzy. His spouse is also upset, and as the shrieking rises to a crescendo, she leaps from the front seat, and the noted Southern editor, a portly man, comes out of the back seat like a bear which has poked its head in a hollow tree and found it inhabited by bees. More smoke boils up and there is one loud and final explosion, at which my friend, who has held to the quarterdeck nobly, like the captain of a sinking ship, himself loses courage and leaps from the car. He lands in my fishworm bed, which is, naturally, a low, swampy place, and from there he can see me on the back porch, doubled up in paroxysms of laughter.

Being a man of quick mind, he naturally sees at once that the whole thing has been a joke and his machine, after all, is not blowing up under his nose.

So he pretends to join in the general merriment, though I can see that his heart is not in it, but he is merely being a good sport. So I bid him an amiable farewell and go on back in the house and curl up with a good book. And along about eleven o'clock I am lying there, at peace with the world. All the children have at last been inspected for ticks and are tucked away, some in their beds, and others down on the floor in sleeping bags, and a great peace lies over the household and nothing disturbs the silent night except the far-away calling of a whippoorwill.

When all of a sudden the whole world seems to explode in one great roaring boom and the windows rattle and kids start diving out of their beds all tangled up in the sheets, and the ones who are on the floor in their sleeping bags take alarm and start scuttling across the floor all tangled up in the bags, and I rise about four feet off the bed and hit the floor running for my shotgun. Then it occurs to me I do not have a shotgun, or any other weapon except a bow and arrow and a Red Ryder BB gun, so I check my original impulse to dash into the night with roars of rage. Instead, I poke my head carefully out the door to reconnoiter, and far away down the mountain I hear the sounds of wild, exultant laughter, and I realize what has happened.

My neighbor down the mountain has borrowed a couple of sticks of dynamite and, aided and abetted by this noted Southern editor, he has set them off about a hundred yards down the road from my house, rattling my windows and scaring me, momentarily, out of my wits. Which makes us even, I suppose, at this point.

Autumn Comes to the Mountains

In the mountains, fall is coming fast. The smell of it is in the air. The look of it is in the hills—that thin golden haze that is the sun shining through a billion billion microscopic particles of drifting pollen. The wind in the morning carries the chill of fall and at night it calls with the voices of fall—the little low moaning sound that is like a puppy whimpering.

The color is coming faintly, the reds and yellows, though the massed hills still wear their summer coat of dusty green. Only along the roadsides, where the low bushes grow, are the fires of fall beginning to flame in all their color.

The drying of the leaves gives a new voice to the mountains. Now when the wind blows, the rustle of the leaves is like the sound of far off surf, a murmur like the murmur of the sea.

All the little creatures are busy this time of year. The chipmunks and the squirrels are in a frantic scurry, packing the acorns and the chinquapins off to their hidden hollows, storing them away for winter. The dead seeds of the weeds and grasses are beginning to travel and the feathery thistles are blowing in the wind. A man who takes a walk now comes back burdened with flat beggar-lice and the little needle-like seeds that have tiny fishhooks on their ends to grab and cling.

The chill of fall is on the waters. At high noon the sun was warm as summer and the lake looked as serene and warm as July. But there was a bite in the water. A man diving in, expecting the blessed coolness of mid-summer, gets a rude shock. The cold water takes his breath and makes his heart jump and pound. A fat man should not celebrate his forty-fifth birthday by diving into a lake in mid-September. He should have more sense than that.

The next two months should be a glorious time in the Southern highlands, a fine time for traveling, for moving about in the hills, all the way from Georgia to Virginia. In another month, or a little less, the woods will be in all their glory. It would be a fine time to take off up the spine of the Blue Ridge, to ride that great highway through the Smokies, the one that follows the high tops all the way. It will be a time to see one of the wildest and most beautiful regions in all America in all the glory of its autumn dress.

The First Fire of Fall

Up here, spring comes late and fall comes early. Already the air is taking on that clear and golden look that is the mark of autumn, and already the first fire has steamed and crackled in the fireplace. The house, open all year to the sweet winds of summer, is snugged tight now, and the smell of wood smoke is in it, the good sharp smell of oak and hickory. A fire feels good in the mornings, and after sunset now, and though there will be more warm days, I know, the heart of summer is beating slowly to a stop.

The cold seems coming on so fast that I am a little worried about a lady whom I greatly admire. She is a little hen partridge, and in a clump of grass down on the slope below the house she is sitting on eight white eggs which ought to be hatching out any day now. I keep wishing she would hurry, for it seems late in the year for little fellows to be coming into the world. It seems to me they should come when the earth is bright with spring and the land itself is being born anew. I guess she knows what she is doing, though, for by the time they come and are big enough to run about, the grasses and the weeds will be dead and dry and dropping their seeds to feed the family. I hope they winter well, for it will be pleasant, next spring, to hear them whistling down in the meadow.

I followed the progress of their father and mother's wooing earlier in the summer, by their calling back and forth to each other, and it was a pleasant sound to hear. It helps a man to do his work somehow, when he can sit and listen now and then to the high, clear whistling of a quail.

The little quail, when they arrive, will not be the only additions to the mountains. The four ducks we put on the lake earlier are seven now. Not long after the first four came, Mr. Lindsey, the Power Company man drove by and saw them, and went home and got three more, a drake and two lady ducks. They didn't get a very warm reception. When he put them in the lake the original four set up a great clamor. The old drake poked his head up in the air and made a great fuss and led his harem off across the lake, flirting his tail from side to side in high dudgeon. The newcomers didn't seem to be disturbed, though. They took out after the original four and swam right along with them, quacking in a friendly manner. The old drake swam at great speed up into the coves and out again, with the other three in hot pursuit. They seem to have settled their differences now, though, and they swim together as a flotilla, seemingly on very friendly terms. But, when somebody goes out on the bridge to feed them, the old drake raises sand if the newcomers try to eat with the family. He fusses and squawks and drives them off until he and his wives have been fed, and then he graciously lets them eat.

The young drake hasn't made any fuss so far about being pushed around this way, but Mr. Baker, down the mountain, who knows something about ducks, says that come spring there is going to be one whale of a duck fight down on the lake, and next year we may see the three new ducks running the show. He says he has been watching the young drake, and he believes his temper is growing short. He says there may be some wife-swapping going on next spring, for one of the old drake's wives has been acting in a very friendly manner to the newcomers, especially to the gentleman newcomer, and that presages trouble.

The ducks seem to know that winter is coming, too, and they appear to be spending more time out on the bank, poking around among the marsh grass where the little stream empties into the lake. They may be finding something to eat there, but I think probably instinct has told them that it is time to be looking for a snug place where they will be shielded from the winter winds.

Sometimes, in years past, wild ducks heading south have stopped off in the fall to visit awhile, and I am anxious to see what the big, fat, tame Pekings are going to do when these wild strangers come whistling in, telling their great tales of far, strange places. I wonder if the tame ducks are going to feel any atavistic yearning to go with the handsome strangers and see the world. Mr. Baker says they won't. But I don't know. It seems to me that life on the lake would seem mighty tame after hearing the boys from the Minnesota marshes talk of their travels.

The mountain has another resident who acts as if he wants to stay. Early in the summer a homeless hound, lean and lank and hungry, wandered in, wagging his whole back end from his ears to the tip of his tail, and snuffling and bobbing his head to indicate that he meant no harm. He's been going around from one house to the other, mooching a meal here and a bed there, and if he ever had a home it seems as if he's forgotten about it. Last night it was cold, with a drizzling rain, and he must have smelled the smoke of the fire, and felt the warmth, for he came in the house, ducking his head apologetically, and lay down by the fire to take a snooze. I am afraid that he has made himself a permanent member of my family, which disturbs me a little, for I do not think that my cat, Chester Junior, is going to stand for that.

One dark and dangerous stranger has left the mountains permanently, to the great relief of all. We let the old rattler out of the cage the other day, and gave him a good start, out across the yard, just so he would have a sporting chance, and then one of the young men who is expert with a pistol shot him, blip, in the back of the neck.

A couple of young medical students happened to be around, so they retrieved him and conducted an autopsy, with the aid of a large volume on anatomy, and found out that snakes and people are made very much the same, both being fearfully and wonderfully fashioned. They seemed fascinated with their study, and spent a whole long afternoon at it, so maybe the old snake did make some contribution to the sum of human knowledge after all. Some folks thought we were foolish to let him live as long as we did, but I'm glad we had him around for the youngsters' sake. They would sit and watch him by the hour, studying his color and the shape of his head, and listening to the strange, dry singing of his rattles. I'll feel a little less worried now when they walk in the woods, for if they ever hear that chilling sound, they'll recognize it immediately, and know enough to get away from there.

An End and a Beginning

The last weekend at the mountain is a sad one sometimes, for over it hangs the shadow of things ending—the end of summer and the golden lazy days, the last walk in the cool of the morning on the rocky road under the trees where the birds no longer sing, the last swim in the cold clear blue-green lake, the last try for the old bass who lives by the drowned stump in the deep cove.

Everything seems clearer and sharper on the last weekend of summer—the last sunset blazes in a greater glory of pink and purple and gold, the last whippoorwill seems to put more heart into his farewell call. Even the slow stars seem to linger in their last march over the mountain down the valley, and the wind sings a softer song as the house settles down for the last cool night of sleep.

But this time it wasn't all that way. When you have a year-old baby around you don't have much chance to lapse into nostalgic dreams. You are seeing a beginning, not an ending. Your thoughts are centered on first things.

The first time she sees a butterfly, his yellow wings winking like gold in the sunshine, and the way she laughs and holds out her hands to it.

The first time she finds a dead candlefly on the window sill, and

picks it up and looks at it solemnly and then pops it in her mouth, and munches happily—until four adults descend upon her, all hollering "Spit it out" and trying to put their fingers in her mouth to fish for it.

The first time she ever saw a body of water bigger than her bathinette, and the wild glee with which she thrashed about in the shallow water at the edge of the lake, arms and legs pumping in an ancient atavistic instinct to swim, while her mama held a supporting hand under her tummy.

The first time she ever walked barefoot in new-cut grass, and tried to follow a drowsy grasshopper on his lazy hops. And the first time she discovered the little ants and bugs and things that live on the ground, which she tried to catch with fat questing fingers.

So this time was a happy time for me because it was a happy time for her, a time for seeing with new eyes, for listening to a new music, for watching a new life unfold.

Fire on the Mountain

I never did get it quite straight. Down in Jasper some said that
the fire started in Gilmer County, near the Whetstone Cove, and
some said it started in Dawson. It was hard to tell, for it was burning along the line where Pickens, Dawson and Gilmer meet, and
it is hard for a man to say for sure just where a county line lies in
the rough uplands of Georgia. Anyway, men came from all
around to fight it, and they fought it without rest for a day and a
half or more and they got it stopped at last at the Cartecay Road,
though it was jumping the road near the Drunkard's Spring when
the rains came, late in the night, and beat it down.

When they finally got it out, 2,500 acres had been burned over.
Grapevine Mountain had burned, and the Redmond, and many
a cove and glen and leafy shade which the deer and turkey and
the pheasant used. The deer got out all right, for they run in
front of a fire. And the turkeys and pheasant flew with the first
stain of smoke on the wind, and the first crackle and roar of the
flame.

But much of the new crop of game was lost, for when Doyle
McWhorter, the Pickens County Fire Warden, and the Mulli-
nax boys, Coleman and Leonard, and Cole Heath, Jr., and
Hardie White, who were in his crew, walked back over the

burned-out land, they found turkey eggs and pheasant eggs baked in the nest. And Lath Pinson and Penny Buffington and the Gilmer County fire rangers said it was the same where they had walked in the woods.

When we got to the house at the mountain a thick mist covered the hills, and through the gray a slow rain was falling. You could see nothing on either side of the road, and only the smell of smoke, still faint in the air, told that the woods had burned. The next morning, though, dawned bright and clear, and with the curtain of mist rolled back, the old mountain back of the house lay there black and charred and dead. From fallen logs wisps of smoke still rose, burning so deep in the punky logs that not even the rain of a night and a day had gotten to the heart of the fire.

Nothing stirred in the charred leaf mold except the lizards, and they behaved strangely. They did not dart and hide, but lumbered along, slowly, and I asked Parks Bearden, who is a mountain man, how the lizards saved themselves, and why they moved about so logily. He said they had burrowed into the ground when the fire came, and the reason they moved slowly now was they had gorged themselves until they could not run. They had come out to find all the creeping and crawling things that live in logs and under leaves baked in their hiding places, and they had almost foundered themselves, like a horse let loose in a corn crib.

You don't understand how fire damages the woods until you get out and walk around where it has burned. The big trees still stand tall and green, and you think that they have not been hurt. But you get up close and look, and you see on the side of the tree where the fire burned hottest, little places where the bark has popped off, as from an inner explosion. Bearden, who fought the fire, said that you could hear these explosions of the heated sap crackling like rifle fire in the woods, and he said that from each place where the bark popped off a spurt of blue flame shot out, as if the heat generated a gas in the tree that burned with a blue-colored flame. A tree, he said, may look as if it had come through a fire all right, but in a few years, he said, you would see it sicken

and begin to die as the borers struck through the places where the bark popped off.

Even the underbrush, the young oaks and the hickories, and the chestnut sprouts that spring up around the old dead stumps, sometimes seem to have come through the fire all right. But if you notice them, you will see that high up, near the top, the bark is split away from the wood, and these young trees, too, will die.

It was a bad fire and only back-breaking work by many men kept it in hand at all. First they fought it against a north wind that carried it as fast as a man could trot, and when they had it stopped, they had to fight it all over again when the wind quartered around to the east and sent it off in a new direction. They saw it crown in the tall, dead chestnuts, and they watched the wind snatch banners of flame from these tall trees and fling them 200 feet, leaping the backfires.

They raked a fire lane for a mile and a quarter, and backfired from it all along the shoulder of the mountain from the Appalachian Trail to the Cartecay Road. And when they brought it out on the Cartecay Road the fire was no more than fifty yards away and the high wind was throwing the flames across the road. But with Mr. Baker, from down the mountain, riding the road, carrying the word where it had jumped, and everybody fighting like killing snakes, they beat out these places where it had crossed. Finally, at 2:45 in the morning, a slow rain began to fall, getting steadier and steadier on toward the day. That stopped it, cold, killing the last little patches of bright flame. And all up and down the road tired firefighters, their eyes sunk deep in their heads, trudged homeward in the rain while mist laid its concealing curtain over the ravaged mountain's wounds.

Problem for Quail Lovers

I knew that partridge hen had no business setting on that
clutch of eggs this time of year. I have been talking to some of my
friends around the mountain about it—old-timers familiar with
the hills and the habits of the game birds and the little animals in
these parts, and they say she is making a big mistake. She will
never raise her brood of young. They will be too small to stand it
by the time the hard cold comes. The way they figure it is she laid
her eggs in May, like any hen partridge with any sense would naturally do, and would have hatched out a covey in June, which is
the normal time for the little quail to appear, if something has
not happened.

They say she probably got broken up—her nest got broken up,
that is—by a prowling fox or maybe a possum. They ate the eggs,
and she, poor soul, still being filled with the maternal instinct,
found her another nest and laid her a batch more eggs, and
started sitting on them.

They say the eggs probably won't even hatch out, because the
cock partridge loses interest in the hens after the spring of the
year, and they figure the eggs are infertile. I don't know how they
know how a cock partridge feels, and what seasons of the year he
feels that way in, but that's what they say.

36

The whole thing troubles me just a little bit. I was hoping she would hatch out and raise herself a nice brood. Nothing in the woods makes a prettier sight than a bunch of tiny quail, hardly bigger than a man's thumb, scooting about after their mother, crossing the road scurrying like little bugs. I was hoping that the old mother quail would be able to hatch and raise her young, so I could see this sight before I leave the mountain. But the way it looks now, these little fellows are going to be about that size when the first freeze comes—they haven't even hatched yet—and they don't have much chance of surviving.

If I knew what to do I would try to take them away from the old lady and raise them as soon as they hatch out. But I have not had any experience feeding baby quail. I would not know whether to try to feed them worms and bugs, like a mother bird, or whether they should have scratch feed, like a baby chicken. I don't know where I could put them, either, where my cat, Chester Junior, would not take an intense—and fatal—interest in them.

Even if I took the little fellows away from their mama, it would probably do nothing but confuse her more. She might lay another setting of eggs and earnestly start sitting on them, even if she had to do so under two feet of snow.

It is a very perplexing problem.

Woodslore—or Folklore

Well, the old hen partridge did know what she was doing. She hatched off the other day. Parks Bearden, from down the mountain, who first found her nest while mowing the golf course, and left a broad swath of high grass so she wouldn't be disturbed, went by to see how she was coming along the other morning and lo and behold there was nothing there but a nest full of shells. Every egg had hatched. So Parks began looking around, knowing that though a partridge moves her young as soon as they hatch, she does not move them far, and sure enough, pretty soon, there went the old bird fluttering and tumbling along as if she were hurt.

He had sense enough to know what she was doing, of course, so he didn't try to follow her. He just stood still and looked around him very carefully, watching where he put his foot, and all around him in the grass he saw the glint of bright little eyes watching him.

The little fellows, no more than a day old, already had learned to sit still where their mother told them to. Parks said he counted at least six, close by where he was standing, and he figured the others were around somewhere, so well hidden by the grasses that he couldn't see them. He was afraid to move about much looking for them for fear he would step on one, so he just came away quietly, watching very carefully where he stepped.

Later that afternoon, as he was riding the tractor down the road, he saw the old hen again, with all her young strung out behind her in a line, crossing the road, and he counted them and found all nine of them to be there. One of them was coming along a little behind the others, he said, and making pretty heavy going of it and when he looked carefully he could see that it had something the matter with one of its feet. He said he started to chase this one and try to catch it, so he could see what was wrong with it, but then he remembered something his father told him years ago, when he was a boy. He had caught a baby partridge that seemed to be crippled and had found that it had a ball of dried mud tightly adhering to its middle toe, bound, seemingly, with wisps of fine grass that made the mud stick goether. He took the little quail to his father to show him this curious thing and his father had explained to him what it was.

His father said that little partridges are just like children. In any group of them there will be one who is headstrong and willful and disobedient who does not pay any attention to what its mother says, and is always strolling off somewhere out of her sight and causing her a great deal of trouble and worry. So the mama partridge fastens this ball of mud around the toe of the headstrong one and it causes him so much trouble that he does not feel like chasing all over the country, investigating things and getting in danger. It makes him limp and stumble, and it is all he can do to keep up with the rest of the covey.

I don't know how much of the story is genuine woodslore, and how much folklore, but Parks says it's so, and he has lived in the woods all his life, and has made a study of the game and the wild things and it may be true that the mother partridge does hamper the more frivolous of her young in this way.

Anyway, what pleases me most is that Parks says there's no use worrying about the old partridge not being able to raise this covey of little ones. She will take care of them all right, he says, even if they were born two or three months later than they were supposed to have been born, and they will come through the winter just fine, unless the woods get dry in the late fall and fire gets out and catches them before they get big enough to fly. They won't mind the cold at all, he says, and when spring comes they will be down in the meadow whistling and calling just as chipper as you please.

I hope that is so, for he promised me that when it comes spring again he is going to teach me to whistle like a lady partridge calling to her mate. He whistled this call for me and it does not sound at all like the familiar "Bob White" call, but is a low, sweet, liquid fluting of very seductive tone. He says we can go up in the woods there and sit down inconspicuously by a tree and whistle this call and every cock partridge on the mountain will answer. He can call them right up to him, he says, so close that you can see the look of indignation which comes over their countenance when they discover that what has been making the seductive whistling sounds is not a lady partridge with matrimonial leanings but a large character wearing overalls. He says you never saw anything as crestfallen as a cock partridge, all dressed up in his finery and strutting like nobody's business, when he steps out of the bushes and sees he has been deceived. He says that he is sometimes afraid they are going to fly at him, in their disappointment and indignation, and peck him on the skull.

I don't know whether that is genuine woodslore or folkslore, either, but come spring I am going to find out.

Little, Friendly Clouds of Home

To me, one of the joys of this place is the privilege it bestows of living on intimate terms with clouds. There are always clouds somewhere in view, great white far-off ones, standing still beyond the mountain top, with the sun shining on them, or small busy gray ones that come trudging past, headed down the valley toward the lake on some business of their own. It is, in some respects, like living in an airplane hanging motionless in the sky, so that the clouds come and go without causing bumpiness or discomfort.

Sometimes I will be sitting here on the front porch, looking out across the valley toward the mountain through air as clear and sparkling as a diamond. Then all of a sudden, here will come a phalanx of clouds, marching down the valley, silent as ghosts, and as little concerned, it seems, as ghosts, with the doings of mortal men.

Sometimes a little one, no bigger than a bed sheet, will come right in the porch, and pause a moment, as if peering in the windows at the light and warmth within. And sometimes a big one comes and wraps the whole house up in its soft gray, and holds it in its heart for half an hour.

It is a welcome visitor, even though as it moves on it does leave things a little damp and clammy. Then kids who have lived in bathing suits all day begin to dig in the bottom of suitcases for sweaters, and people red with sunburn experience that strange sensation of burning and shivering at the same time, as the feverish skin contracts into goose bumps in the damp and cold.

When you are very close to a cloud, when it is in fact all around you, it lacks the appearance of beauty. You can only feel its soft, cool dampness. It has no contour, no outline. The nice ones to look at are the far off ones, the ones that drift above and beyond the mountain.

There is no factory smoke up here to stain and sully the air, so the far-off skies are a very clear blue, and the clouds are of a wondrous whiteness like this manufactured whipped cream that squirts from cans.

They form great cloud cities in the sky, complete with skyscrapers, and little houses, and streets and highways—cities that are not static in shape or form, but always changing, even though the eye can see no movement.

And I sometimes think that the most beautiful cloud formations in all the world are those that drift here where the Appalachian chain ends and the big mountains break off suddenly to flow in rolling Piedmont hills, past Atlanta to the flat lands of the South.

Remembering the great cloud masses that rise above the green islands of the Pacific, beacons of beautiful mist that are mileposts for the navigators, and the towers of cloud that rise pink and gold above the Andes in the mornings, and the wondrous formations that drift above the Mediterranean, I know that this is not so.

But these are the clouds that drift above the hills of home. These are the little friendly clouds that come silently in the windows and drift quietly out again. That makes the difference.

One Summer's Journey— From Baby Pool to Deep Water

The first day was the kind you dream about, when you are thinking about vacations. High blue skies with clouds adrift, and enough wind to make the water dance in little waves, and the water blue, and so clear that six feet straight down you can see your feet, and cold, but not too cold. Just the first chill when you dive in and then not cold, not warm, but just right—except when you swim through those special places where cold streams feed in a flow of icy water beneath the surface, water pouring out of the deep rocks of the hills with the breath of winter in it.

It is one of the minor pleasures of the place—here, actually, all pleasures are minor—to watch a visiting swimmer, unforewarned, strike one of the places where the icy springs pour in and to hear them shout in anguish and surprise and thrash the water mightily.

It was one of those days when all the mamas were out with all their young, including their youngest young, some of whom were so small they could not even yet sit up so that their mothers had to hold them under the arms, dunking them gently in the water. For it is understood that babies are never too small to be dunked in these waters. You start as soon as they are born, sitting with

44

them in the shallows while they splash, and then in a little while they are sitting alone and in a season are moving into the middle deeps, where the water is up to their navels.

Here they learn to put their heads under and splash with their arms and kick. And then they move out where the waters are up to their chins or a little over and they play there while their mamas watch. And now it is time for them to start diving. So the mamas stand their young on the dock while they stand in the water. And the small fry start by lunging bravely off the dock into their mothers' arms. And then they lunge off into the water, their mamas catching them as they go under.

Pretty soon they are plunging head first off the dock with no one there to catch them. This is the "Look, Mama, look at me," stage which lasts for a season. Then all of a sudden they are out of the baby pool and the middle waters and are over in the deep, where everybody swims—the teen-agers and the grownups and all. And they are plunging thirty feet off the top tower, who a year before were timidly jumping from the dock into their mamas' arms.

And it is a good thing to lie, dozing on the dock in the hot sun, watching a new generation come along to know the joy of this quiet spot where nobody does anything he does not want to do, which means that nobody does anything much, except doze and dream and seek the sun and, for a little while, know peace.

The Phoebes Just Took Over

The two fledgling phoebes which lived on the front porch have finally flown and everybody is breathing a little easier now. They were a great responsibility while they were with us, and something of a nuisance, because their parents were of a nervous type who would fly into a state of great alarm every time anybody walked out on the porch. They had some reason to be agitated, of course, because you know how kids are. The presence of a bird nest on the front porch whets their curiosity to a fever heat, and they have to be shinnying up the post all the time to peer into the nest to see how the eggs are coming along, and whether or not they have started to hatch yet, and this always agitates the mama phoebe considerably, who will flit from the nest uttering loud peeps of distress, which in turn would perturb her husband, and the two of them would buzz about peeping their heads off.

This did not matter so much on warm days, but it was a matter of some concern when it was cloudy and cold, for there was a good chance that the eggs would get chilled and would not hatch if the mama stayed off the nest too long at a time.

Fortunately, though, this did not happen and both of the eggs hatched out and the young people in no time at all were sitting up there cheeping lustily and yelling for food at all hours. So I got the children together and gave them a good lecture about not climbing up to the phoebes' nest to peer at the little birds, because this would interrupt their feeding routine, the mama bird being afraid to return with worms if somebody was always shinnying up the post peering into the nest just about the time she arrived. They were pretty reasonable about it, and were content merely to peek out from behind the screen door, watching the mama and papa phoebe bringing worms to their young.

The presence of the young birds, tweeting and chirping and carrying on, had a very bad effect on my cat, Chester Junior, though. While there was nothing but eggs in the nest Chester Junior paid it little attention, but as soon as the little birds arrived all his hunting instincts were aroused and he would sit for hours peering up at the nest until I am positive he got a crick in his neck. Sometimes when he thought no one was looking he would try to jump up to the nest, but it was too high, and whenever anybody heard him jumping they would go out and whack him with a folded newspaper, causing him to leap off the porch and flee into the bushes in high dudgeon. Finally he decided just to leave them alone.

The presence of the birds caused a considerable change in the habits of the household, too, for the only place to sit in the cool of the afternoon and have a good view of both the mountain and the lake was on the end of the porch directly under the corner where the nest was located, and while people were sitting there the mama and papa phoebe would not bring food to their young. They would go off and catch a huge fat worm and come back and light on the dead limb of an oak near the porch and sit there with the worm, much distraught. You could see them trying to make up their minds to come on in with the worm and sometimes they would brace themselves and dart in and almost light at the nest but their courage would always fail them at the last moment and they would dart back to the dead limb.

Finally, not wishing to take over the feeding of the phoebes myself, worms being hard to come by around here, I decided that the only thing to do was to give up that corner of the front porch.

So with vast physical exertion I moved the glider and the chairs and the table over to the other end of the porch, which is a fairly long porch, and everybody sits there in the cool of the afternoon, while the phoebes take over the other end and feed their young in peace.

But nobody enjoyed sitting at this end of the porch for the late sun would beat in with a great glare, and when visitors were present they would sit there shading their eyes and mopping their brows, and finally they would inquire what was the sense of sitting in the sun parboiling when the other end was so shady. They would look at me a little queerly, I'm afraid, when I would explain that a family of phoebes had taken up their residence at the other end and that I was trying to insure them privacy in which to raise their young.

So it was a great day when the little ones finally staggered up to the edge of the nest and sat there teetering in alarm, and finally took off, flogging the air furiously on their solo flight. They came back once or twice, but as their wings grew stronger and their confidence in themselves increased, their absences from the nest grew longer and longer, and now they do not come back to the old homestead at all.

Which suits me just fine, and I hope that next year they will move in on somebody else.

Of Phoebes, Mice and Rabbits

They didn't, though. That mama phoebe is back again this spring to confuse and bewilder me, and this time I am going to be firm with her. Things have come to a pretty pass when a man cannot walk out on his own front porch and sit down and put his feet up on the rail and sit there tranquilly, contemplating the blue distances of the mountain and the sheen of the sun on the lake without having a little bird no bigger than his thumb heap maledictions upon him and whirl about his head as if she were going to light on his skull at any moment and peck a hole in it.

Last year I let that phoebe bluff me. I walk out on the front porch happily, breathing deeply of the fine clear air, and she starts whirling and darting around until I retreat behind the screen to keep her from assaulting me. Peering through the screen, I see what the cause of all the trouble is. She has built her nest in the corner of the porch, right up under the porch roof, and she has laid her eggs in this nest and is determined that nothing is going to happen to keep her from raising a happy little family.

So I give orders that nobody shall sit on the corner of the porch where the phoebe makes her residence, and I wallop the kids every time they try to climb up the post to peer into the nest, and

I even move the glider over to the other end of the porch, so that the phoebe will not be disturbed by people sitting near her nest.

This year I have taken a different tack. I have moved the glider back over to the shady side right under the phoebe's nest and I am going to sit there. I am not going to bother the phoebe nor her young and she might as well find it out and get used to having me around. I am going to buy me a derby hat, and a pair of welder's glasses, for protection, and I am going to put on the derby and the glasses and let her do her worst. I will just sit there and let her wear herself out, making no effort to defend myself. Maybe she will then calm down and go on and sit on her nest and raise her young'uns and quit getting in such a dither.

I have not yet decided what to do with the mouse which has made his residence in the tool shed. I am very fond of this mouse. He is a little bright-eyed fellow with large dark brown eyes and a very perky moustache. His nest, built of grasses and slender vines, sits right inside the doorway to the tool shed and every time I go in the tool shed he pops his head out in great alarm and as soon as he sees me he utters a frightened squeak and goes bumping out the back door of his nest and down through a crack in the floor.

I hate to frighten him this way, but if he will just stick around he will learn I do not wish to harm a single whisker he possesses and he can go on living there, rent free, as long as he wishes. He is a brown woods mouse, and I am the implacable enemy of only the common gray, or house mouse.

I may have to do something about him yet, though, for my neighbor down the lake, a banker of great dignity and reserve, sometimes enters my tool shed to borrow a rake or a spade, and he has rebuked me sharply about allowing wild animals to infest it.

This year I was careful to tell him about the mouse's nest in the tool shed, and he approached it whistling blithely. In about a minute, though, I hear a hoarse shout of alarm, and I look up to see my friend the banker leap through the door of the tool shed and lope across the yard at great speed.

"What's the matter?" I said, "I told you there was a mouse's nest in there, just about level with your head as you stepped in."

"Yes," he said, wiping the moisture from his spectacles. "But you neglected to inform me that there was a mouse in the nest. I step in and stand there a moment, getting my eyes accustomed to the gloom, and about two inches from my nose I see two beady eyes glaring at me. Also, I am positive I heard him growl fiercely as I departed."

I also am puzzled about what to do about four other little furry creatures who inhabit my estate. I go out the other morning and with great travail clean off and spade up a place about the size of a Pullman berth, and there I plant a fine garden. I put in beans and carrots and turnips and radishes and I don't know what all. Then, just as I am finishing my labors and am mopping the honest sweat from my brow, I look down at my feet. There is a little wisp of fur there, and some bits of grass.

As I stand there observing, I suddenly leap about three feet in the air, for the spot covered by this fur and grass is palpitating slowly, as if something alive had stirred beneath it. Mustering my courage, I poke about with a stick for a moment, and sure enough, there is a small, bright eye peering up at me. I poke the entrance to the nest a little wider, and peer in again and there, bless my soul, are four baby rabbits, each one just about big enough to cuddle in the palm of your hand.

I call Mr. Baker, who is my advisor on matters having to do with the flora and fauna of the mountains, and he comes and observes the baby rabbits. I ask him how old he thinks these rabbits are, and how soon they will be able to get out and rustle around for themselves, for I am afraid that their mama will not come back to nurse them if she notes that the nest has been disturbed.

"She'll come back all right," said Mr. Baker. "And she may even move them, though I doubt it. As for their age. Well, from what I know of rabbits and garden patches, I figure that just about two minutes after the first bean plant pops up out of the ground in your garden, the first of these rabbits will pop up out of this hole, ready to eat it. Yes, sir, I would say that you and that mama rabbit timed everything just about right."

The White Heron Couldn't Stay

A tall and beautiful white heron dropped in at the lake the other day and everybody hoped that he, or she, would like the place well enough to stay—maybe bringing in a mate later on, and raising a family. A few of the young folks who like to get out on the lake at night, hunting frogs, were a little perturbed for fear the frog population would be decimated, depriving them of a good excuse to float about on the lake in a canoe, by moonlight, but those of us who have given up such enterprises were glad the bird had come, and did not begrudge him the frogs. A chorus of frogs at night is fine for soothing the nerves and lulling one to slumber, and it is a mild pleasure to shoot them, and to eat the frog legs. But the general consensus was that the sight of the crane, or heron, or whatever, was worth more than the frogs he might consume.

It was a pleasure to watch him, standing in the shallows, his long yellow spear of a beak poised ready to flash down whenever a minnow darted around his ankles, or a frog hopped too near.

It turned out, though, that our white friend was not to be with us long. Somewhere, before he arrived here, some lunkhead with a shotgun and no brains had tested his marksmanship on him, and the poor fellow had a shattered leg. He evidently had managed to keep in flight after the charge struck, and had made it here, a quiet spot where he evidently hoped to recover.

There was no sign he was wounded the first day, for he stood in the shallows all day, fishing, evidently with fair luck. But the first night, when the frog hunters were on the lake, he took fright, and strangely, instead of flying into the woods, he headed for a house that sat by the edge of the lake. Soft as a shadow floating he flew into the yard and lit, and stood there, observing the people on the porch without fear.

Nobody made any move toward him, for fear he would be frightened, so he just sat there. Once or twice he tried to move about a bit, and then it was noticed that he stumbled, and fell, and had difficulty getting up again on his long reed-like legs, the right one going off in a funny direction until he could get up on the left and pull it up under him.

He sat there quite a while until the cat, coming around the side of the house, spotted him, and, creeping up swiftly with his tail twitching, leaped at him before anybody could make a move. The cat missed his spring by inches, but the bird had great trouble taking off, for his wounded leg would not function. He flew off into the shadows though, and the next morning the kids walking to the dock reported that he was standing beside the road, and that he looked all right, though he did not move when they passed almost in reach of him. Later that day, he was seen in the marshy shallows, trying to fish, but he seemed to be having trouble keeping his balance, and later he was seen to sink into the marsh and struggle up, the white feathers of his breast all muddy.

By late afternoon he was definitely down, so a couple of us went over and waded out and picked him up and brought him in to see if there was anything that could be done. There wasn't, for between the leg and the body were the blue holes where the shot went in, and beneath the skin you could feel the grating of the broken bone.

There were a couple of premedical students on the mountain that weekend, so they laid him out very gently, and tried to set his leg and put a splint on it. But a crane's leg, even high up against the body, is like a toothpick, and there was no way you could strap it or splint it to make it immovable. The funny thing was, he seemed to know that we were trying to help him, for, though he could move his head around, he did not struggle, and though his beak could have plucked out an eye if he had struck with it, he made no effort to peck anybody.

We fed him a little, and laid him out with the leg stretched out, and wrapped him in a towel and put him in a box near an electric light, so he would keep warm, hoping that maybe he would make it through the night. He had put up such a fight to live, there was some chance that his leg might heal if he were fed by hand, and kept quiet.

But the next morning he was dead. And I guess the jerk who shot the wild and beautiful thing, if he sees this, will be proud to know that he didn't miss, after all.

First You Sleep, Then You Walk and Look and Listen

In New York the other day a friend, who'd heard me sounding off at lunch about the mountain and the lake and how quiet it was there, gave what sounded very much like a snort of derision.

"Yes," he said, "but what do you do to keep from going out of your mind with boredom?"

I'd never thought about it much. But it was a good question. So I tried to answer.

Well, I said, first, you sleep. It's cool and quiet, so quiet you can hear the little borers gnawing in the wood of the old house— so quiet you can hear the rustle of a mouse trotting through the leaves outside. So you sleep and you get up early and walk down a dirt road that winds through woods and by open meadows and over little streams and past little ponds. And as you walk you look and listen.

You look at all the little tracks in the dusty places, where bugs and lizards and all the little things that creep about in the night have passed. And sometimes you see where a coon has walked, or a doe and her fawn have come down to a still pond to drink.

And you listen and you hear a hundred different bird songs you can't identify and a hundred squeaks and rustlings and hums and buzzings. And you stop by a pond and watch black clusters of tadpoles just coming from the long beads of black shiny eggs in the shallows.

Then you come to the lake, and you peel down to your shorts and lie on the old weathered planks, hot in the morning sun, and you drop little bits of broken bread in the water and watch the little fishes come to eat them. And sometimes you can see, deep down in the clear water, a big bass trying to get his courage up to come up and eat a little fish.

Then you walk back, not on the road, but on the old golf course fairways now grown up wild. And here you look at tiny little yellow flowers and little waxy blue flowers. And sometimes if you look close you can see a tiny white violet no bigger than half your little fingernail.

And a meadow lark flies up and you know her nest is there. So you circle carefully around the place she flew from and pretty soon you see a dark shadowy place like a tiny cove in the tufted grass. And you walk up close enough to see the four tiny eggs in their nest of grass.

And all that takes up a morning. And then you eat and sleep awhile through the heat of the day, and then you go sit on the front porch and watch a black butterfly taking his nourishment from the pink blossom of the wild honeysuckle that grows beside the house.

Or you sit very still while a sweat bee hangs in front of your nose, and you wonder how his whirring wings can hold him motionless in the air. And you watch a hunting hawk, and you notice that all the bird songs stop until he has gone by.

Then, when the sun goes down and the coves of the lake fall into dark shadow and the birds that have been quiet in the hot afternoon begin to sing again, you go down to the lake and get in a boat and let the evening wind drift you along the banks, where the wild azaleas glow like orange flames in the dark.

And sometimes you catch a fish or two and sometimes you don't, but you don't much care. For it is good to be out on the quiet water, smelling the sweet-shrub along the banks, smelling the rank primeval smell that comes from the water itself where the bream are bedding, where the mama bream are laying their eggs and the buck bream are fertilizing them with milt.

And you go home in the dark to sit on the porch and watch the moon rise, until the whippoorwills begin to chorus and it's time to sleep again.

And I guess it is pretty boring, come to think about it. But somehow I never found it so.

They Found the Ducks a Home

In the dead of night a young friend of mine from down the mountain comes by my house, looking sheepish.

"I have a present for you," he said, with a smile which looks as if it is meant to allay suspicion. He goes to the back of the ancient machine which he drives, one of the earlier examples of the auto manufacturer's art, and raises the lid to the trunk. I peer in. A large white duck with a long neck and a yellow eye is peering at me in a displeased manner. He utters the web-footed equivalent of a Bronx cheer, flirts his tail from side to side, and ignores me. Three smaller ducks, which I gather are the members of his harem, take their cue from their lord and master and do the same.

"My young friend," I say, "I am deeply fond of you, and I trust, of course, that you are equally as fond of me. But there is more to this than meets the eye. Just why are you going about in the moonlight with the back end of your car loaded with barnyard fowl? What are the facts in this case?"

Well, it seems that this is what has happened. He has gone down to Marietta to visit his girl friend, and while there had made the grave error of admiring the ducks which are squonking and quacking around in the backyard. Whereupon his girl friend's father has leaped from his chair, seized him by the hand, pumped it heartily, and made him a present of the ducks. It seems that the old gentleman does not care for these ducks, due to their habit of making loud noises early in the mornings, and indulging in much bickering among themselves while he is trying to take a nap in the afternoons after lunch.

My young friend is an amiable soul, with any young man's natural awe of his girl friend's father, and he lacks the experience and poise necessary to handle such a situation. He does not see any way he can gracefully refuse when a man whom he wishes to please in all respects offers him four ducks. So he accepts them with thanks.

All the way back up the mountain, though, with the ducks honking and squacking in the back of the car, he ponders what to do with them. His own father, he knows, will not hold these ducks in any higher esteem than did the sire of his girl friend. In fact, he knows if he shows up at the house with four ducks, he will run a grave risk of being tossed out on his ear, ducks and all. So he brings them to me.

Naturally, after he explains all this to me, my heart bleeds for him, so I ponder the matter and come up with a solution. We will just present the local colony-at-large with the ducks. We will take them down to the lake and turn them aloose and say nothing about it, and when the other people see the ducks they will think probably they are just some local ducks which have wandered over the mountain to make their residence here.

So we make up a big batch of corn meal dough and feed the ducks and then we take them down to the lake and launch them. They set up a great outcry when we take them out of the car, but as soon as they hit the water you've never seen happier ducks. The three lady ducks snuggle up close to the gentleman duck and they take off, swooping this way and that upon the water as if they are moving to the strains of the "Skater's Waltz," chattering to themselves in an excited manner.

And instead of being enraged when he sees the ducks paddling about on the lake in front of his house, my young friend's father is entranced. He now sits on his front porch all day with a set of binoculars and watches the ducks as they swim about and he finds their activities fascinating. This, of course, is a gross invasion of the ducks' privacy, but he learns a great deal about the habits of ducks from his research.

In fact, all of the local denizens seem pleased that the ducks are here, and are not upset by the prediction of my friend with the binoculars that, from his observation, there is a strong possibility that before long there will be so many ducks available that the association can declare an annual dividend of two ducks per householder, for eating purposes.

Something Cried Out in the Nighttime

My hope that the wild things, other than woods mice and rabbits, would come back to the hills seems to be coming to fulfillment. A neighbor, from down the road, reported the other morning that when he went up to inspect the level of water in the drouth-depleted reservoir, he was barked at by a fox.

A little later the same day my friend Dr. Roper, from down at Jasper, reported that as he was driving up the mountain, a pair of red fox cubs stood on the high bank by the side of the road looking curiously at him as he passed. They did not bark at him nor make any other threatening gesture, and since they did not seem to be in need of medical attention he did not stop. He said they looked about half grown, and would indubitably be able to give somebody's dogs a fine race in about another year.

I am greatly pleased to learn that foxes have been heard barking in these parts, and that fox cubs have been seen. I am not a great admirer of deer hunters, who chase deer with dogs and shoot does and fawns indiscriminately, but the fox hunter is a different breed of man.

The fox hunter is apt to be a philosopher. He has a fine ear for music, and he loves the night and the woods and the sound of the chase.

I contemplate with pleasure sitting on my porch up here some night, when the woods are moist and a slipping fox leaves a breast-high scent, listening to the chorus as the bellmouth dogs and the squallmouth dogs and the chopmouth dogs give a big red a run through the hills.

And I hasten to add, for the benefit of my friends who belong to the SPCA, that there is no element of cruelty in these chases. Fox hunting as it is done in these hills is not a blood sport as it is in England, where the kill is the climax of the chase.

In the Southern mountains, the chase itself is the thing, and there is reason to believe that the fox himself gets as much fun out of baffling the dogs, as the hunters get out of sitting by their fires on the ridgetops, sipping from fruit jars full of corn squeezings and listening to the music of the hounds.

Another friend of mine does not completely share my joy that the wild things are returning to this part of the hills. He was, he said, sitting at a friend's house the other night when something occurred which still causes his eyes to bulge slightly, and the hair to stand up on his head like porcupine quills.

He was sitting quietly, he said, listening to the great orchestra of the night playing soft and sweet and low, when all of a sudden upon the evening air there came a shriek, a screech, a wail that caused his heart to stop, his posterior to leave the chair in which he was sitting and his epidermis to break out in goose pimples as big as a bantam's eggs.

It was, he said, like the cry of some poor lost soul wailing from the nethermost depths of the pit, a shriek like that of a woman in mortal agony. The sound of it hung upon the air for a moment and then it was followed by an angry, snarling bark, something like the bark of a dog, yet still not quite like a dog. On the heels of this barking came again the unearthly screech, and after that a sort of whimpering sound.

My friend, not being exactly a John Burroughs in the woods, cannot explain what made this sound. He has pondered over it—though the memory of it still makes him break out in cold perspiration even when he contemplates it in broad daylight—and he can't figure it out.

He has finally come to the conclusion that the wildcat which has been seen in these parts of late came upon the fox cubs seen by Dr. Roper on the road and did them mortal harm. The barking sound, he thinks, was the dog fox, or perhaps the vixen, berating the wildcat for its assault upon their young.

He has suggested that I, being a younger man, stronger in wind and limb than he, should go into the rocky dell from which the wild cries emanated and there see if I could find any sign of what took place.

It is not that I am afraid of wildcats, of course, for everybody knows that a wildcat is a great coward and will run away at high speed when confronted by a person. but somehow I have not gotten around to this.

The Sun Comes Back to the Mountain

The sun finally came back to the mountain to stay awhile, and brought as its gift as fine and fair a weekend as I can remember. I got up very early one morning to watch it work. It was busy drying up the million billion dew drops that give a diamond glisten to the grass of the old golf course.

It warmed the backs of the thousand little frogs that sat on twig and stone and grassy hummock around the banks of the little pond, and it seemed to put the tadpoles in the shallows into a sort of frenzy. It burned away the mists that drifted above the surface of the big lake, and striking deep into the clear water, it seemed to put the bass out of their minds.

At least they bit better than I remember them at a shiny bit of plastic shaped like a minnow, that I offered them for breakfast, and three of them, plump with fat, came home to make my breakfast, the best fish I've caught in so short a time since I don't know when.

It shone in burnished gold all day and when it went down in a glory of colored cloud over the blue mountains to the west, it pulled a huge moon after it over the other rim of the world.

The moon, so big it seemed about to fill the eastern sky at the head of the valley, had about as much of a dizzying effect on the people as did the sun on the tadpoles and the little creatures of the morning. Until late in the night canoes were on the lake, and from over by the dock came the sounds of guitars strumming and people singing, soft and low.

I was too tired and sleepy and sun-soaked to do any singing but, bemused by the magic of the night, Mama and I did get a blanket and go down to the middle of the meadow and lie there for a long time, watching the big moon rise and diminish and turn from deep burnt gold to silvery white.

We stayed there in the pool of light that filled the valley, listening to the whippoorwills and the bullfrogs down by the pond, until the ground fog rose and began to drift like smoke, and the dew began to fall.

Then we walked back to the house, chilled and feeling a little foolish at having done so silly a thing. But happy, too.

A Young Fawn Dies

There was great excitement, and a great sorrow, at my house a little while ago, and it will be a long time before the littlest kids, at least, are happy again.

The house, which is an old mountain house, sits on the side of a hill, beneath some oak trees, broken and battered by the winter storms. In front of it is a stretch of open land that once was the lawn-smooth fairway of a golf course, but which is now grown up in weeds and many-colored wild flowers.

Beyond this open space is a deep thicket of alders and sumac, and tangled briers, and sourwood, running along the banks of a little stream, and beyond the stream is the huge mass of what the old timers used to call Burnt Mountain, in memory of a great fire which swept it fifty-odd years ago.

And nobody ever goes into the tangled thicket along the stream, or climbs the steep brushy slope of the mountain, and whatever wild things live there live out their lives undisturbed. Hawks float there on still wings by day, and by night it is the haunt of the big owls, who cry in the dark.

Well, this morning, down by the edge of the thicket, my oldest one was chopping down a tree into fireplace wood when all of a sudden, out of the thicket, came a little cry. Sometimes it sounded like a baby crying in pain and terror, and sometimes it sounded like a cat.

So we ran into the thicket, toward the sound of the crying, and there on the ground was my dachshund, Shim, with his jaws clamped hard around the slim body of a little spotted fawn. We beat him off, and I picked up the little deer, and brought it to the house. And as I carried it across the meadow to the house, with all the kids running and crying "What is it—What is it?", I could feel its heart beating and it kicked and turned a little in my arms.

But as I laid it down on the bed, with the kids running to bring towels to wrap it in, it stiffened and its eyes glazed, and it died. There was hardly a mark on it—just one little place on its side where the dog's teeth had pierced the skin. I think it must have died of fright more than anything else. And I don't think old Shim really was trying to kill it. I think he was just trying to bring it to the house to show us what he had caught.

It's a pity the little fellow didn't run, for Shim is fat, and low slung, and he couldn't catch a healthy turtle, and he hasn't got sense enough, so far as I have ever seen, to track an elephant in the snow. But a mother deer teaches her babies to lie still, for they have no odor, and their only protection is the dappling of their hide which makes them blend against the leaves in perfect camouflage. And they lie there hidden, but in plain view, while wildcats and other predators pass by.

And I think old Shim, prowling around in the thicket, must have just blundered up on the deer purely by accident, and grabbed it.

We whipped Shim, and scolded him, and right now he's creeping about the house looking mournful, with his head down, and a shamed look about him.

Nobody will stay mad at him long, I know. But I hope the next time he goes down in that thicket, nosing around, the old deer sees him and gives him a good going over with her sharp hooves. Or he comes up on a good-sized wildcat who is feeling in no mood to be pushed around by little fat, underslung dogs.

That ought to teach him a lesson.

Beauty—A Strange Thing

North of Ball Ground there was ice on the trees, the first ice, and under the dull, gray sky the land looked dead and cold as the old year died. But the roads were clear and traffic still moved so we pushed on to Jasper, where the man at the filling station put the chains on, looking a little dubious, for mountain folk don't like to go to chains until the snow gets deep, because the chains bite into the tires.

Then we turned right, over the paved state road, and began the nine-mile-climb to the top of the mountain. And to tell the truth, we four city slickers did feel a little foolish, clanking along there with chains on while the cars from the mountain counties, Pickens and Gilmer and Dawson and Union, whizzed along unshod.

Then we nervous flat-landers began to feel better for as we passed the turn-off to Bent Tree, and Grand View Lake, and the Salvation Army camp, the blue-steel of ice began to show on the roads here and there, and in the deep cuts, where the roadbuilders had blasted through solid stone, the long gray icicles hung down from the jagged rocks like the beards of forest giants of ancient times. And we were no longer embarrassed by our chains, for now and then a car with a high-number tag would whiz

71

past and hit an icy spot ahead and do a sashay right toward the
ditch and an allemand left toward the cliff, with the man at the
wheel fighting to straighten her out.

So, with the chains taking a solid bite we drove on through
spitting snow that came at the windshield like feathery bullets,
and beside the road little gray birds with fluffed up feathers flit-
ted in the roadside kudzu, black and frost-killed and glazed with
ice.

Then the falling snow thinned and was gone, for we were riding through the last expiring breath of the great storm that on
the night before had dropped its uncountable tons of snow over
all the mountain tops. It was like the snow caps you see on calen-
dars. Up to 2500 feet or thereabout there was no snow, but from
there on up trees bent under the white blanket and under the
trees it was deep.

We turned off the paved road, and down the icy ramp over the
dam, and onto the curving road around the lake, which lay darkly
glimmering, like blue-green slate—a polished stone set in snowy
cusps of the surrounding hills. Then finally we came to the end of
the road, and there was the little house that Mae Perkins and Bill
and Mama and I had come so far to find, a far-off place where
four old friends could spend a quiet New Year's Eve.

In all the years we'd been coming here I'd never seen it like
this. Once there had been an ice storm. But that had been black
and silver and cruel with a biting wind. But this was all softness,
all white stillness. Framed against the background of the snowy
hills, which I remembered only in full leaf, sitting at the edge of a
great snow-meadow which I remembered only in the green of
spring or the gold and crimson of autumn wildflowers, the little
house under its snow blanket looked both familiar and unfamil-
iar, like the snow scene on somebody else's Christmas card.

We stood there, looking down the valley where a ray of late
sun was breaking through to fill the low places with purple
shadows and touch the ridgelines with a gold and crimson shimmer. And about this time Lamar Dunn, the wiry little mountain
man who looks after the places up here, came bounding up in the

pickup truck to see if we were all right. And we said to him almost in chorus, "Lamar did you ever see anything so beautiful in all your life."

And Lamar, who with his wife Josie lives up here the year round, and sometimes in the winter never sees blue sky or the brown earth for six weeks at a time, looked down the snowy valley and up the slopes where the trees bent under the burden of snow. And he spat in the snow, and uttered what was in his heart:

"You all mus' be out of your minds," he said.

Wild Winds and Dancing Deer

Late in the afternoon of that warm and cloudy second day there came a shift in the wind from south to the northwest. The clouds which had defied the sun all day began to break into rags and tatters. In massed battalions they marched up over the crest of the mountains, driven by the wind, breaking before the wind, hurrying before the wind like gray elephants stampeding. Soon the sky was blown clear and blue, and in the place of the ghostly silence that had held the valley in its grip, there was a deep, low murmuring, a whispering that rose to a moaning roar and fell to a sigh. Over the ridge and down the valley the wind raced, bending the trees, setting the broken branches swaying. The red clay roads, slippery under the slow drizzle of the morning and the midday, began to dry and harden. The fire in the fireplace lifted up its red dancing banners and began to sing. Smoke poured from the chimney, whipping away along the wind, and logs that had steamed and simmered all day burned with a hot flame that leaped high up the throat of the chimney.

The sun went down in a blaze of blue and gold, but the evening silence, the time when all the world seems to pause for breath, did not come. Night brought a lift in the voices of the wind, a high moaning note. Leaves raced along the ground and all

74

the forest-covered hills were alive with the twisting and the bending of the trees.

It was New Year's Eve, and in the rush of the wind, pouring along beneath a sky filled with racing clouds, we went out in a spatter of cold and driving rain that came and went with the passing of the clouds. In a clear moment we drove down toward the lake, and off to the right of the road, in an open meadow, the lights of the car fell on the white flags of three deer. A buck and his does, they seemed, though in the dim light it was hard to tell. They watched for a moment, and then paid us no more attention. Leaping and running, dancing and bounding, they went on with their play in the windswept meadow, in the blast of the hurrying wind. We went on, and again in the lights, alone and proud, we saw another deer. She watched a moment and then she went away, with a strange lurch to her bouncing run. It was the famous three-legged doe of the mountain, crippled by a hunter. Her strange hoof-prints are known to the mountain folks around, and they feel for her a sympathy and a pity.

And then we went on, to hear from a boy at the house down the road the story of the night, not long ago, when he was coming home late, and on the hill above him had heard a wild and terrifying scream, like the hysterical screech of a woman insane, which he thinks was the cry of a panther.

It was good that night to sleep with the chuckle of the fire in the chimney and the howl of the great wind outside, beating at the doors, slamming broken limbs from the crippled trees against the side of the house. It is always good, in a strange place, after hearing stories of panthers which walk abroad and scream, to sleep with a big wind blowing. All strange noise then can be blamed on the wind, and a man can lie there, warm and drowsy, and unalarmed by whatever creatures, real or imaginary, may walk the night.

The next day the wind had done its work. The trees were bare of the dead and twisted limbs they had carried since the great ice storm some years ago. The last vestige of heat and rain and fog and cloud had been blown from the sky, and the morning was

75

clear and clean and bright and bitter cold—a very fine morning indeed to mark the start of a year.

The Right-On Generation

I am a naive fellow by nature, but I think that the younger generation, taking them for all in all, are a lot better than we think they are, and I am going to quit worrying about them.

On New Year's Eve, for example, I made my way to an old friend's house in the mountains expecting to find there the same old crowd I'd foregathered with on this occasion for many years. And I'd gone expecting to drink the same old hackneyed toasts, sing the same old sentimental threadbare songs, tell the same old jokes.

But this time the wintry blasts and icy roads had thwarted all but the most fool-hardy of the elders. One family had been wrecked on the highway, being very nearly done in by a skidding chickenfeed truck. Others, showing the erosion of confidence that comes with advancing age, had chickened out, sending their regrets over the thin and shaking telephone system that gives the listener the feeling that he is being shouted at over a kudzu vine.

So I walked in out of the snow into a room where around the simmering fire in the big rock fireplace was gathered a throng of young people, twenty or more, male and female, most of them cousins, ranging in age from nine to nineteen, or thereabout, give or take a year or two at either end. And the first thing I noticed

77

was that though there was a smell of wood smoke in the room, I didn't detect at all the sweetish smell of pot, though these were supposedly members of the turned-on generation.

And I also noticed that whatever alcohol was being drunk, was being drunk by the relatively small number of elders in the room. And I further took note that the only beard in the house was not worn by an under-thirty youth, but by my well-over-forty host. And the only hair that was so long it curled over the ears, curled over ears that belonged to a mature newsmagazine reporter and an aging newspaper columnist.

The songs, too, were not what I would have expected. The eardrum-piercing decibels of hard rock were absent. There was a singer and a guitar, but the singer did not grunt and gasp as if he was being hit in the solar plexus. The music was somehow reminiscent of the chansons of the Middle Ages, the balladry of wandering troubadours. It was sweet and plaintive and in a minor key.

These were not "square" young people in any sense. They all had been brought up in very permissive families. They were sharply intelligent, highly sophisticated. They were poised and self-assured; there were no gigglers and foot-shufflers among them; they were in their own special meaning of the word, cool.

And I may be hopelessly naive about this, but I don't think so. I think that what I have seemed to have sensed is true—the rebel generation is beginning to calm down a little, to grow a little weary of revolt in its more raucous manifestations, to find no particular point any more to shouting "Right On," when nobody quite knows the answer to the question "Right On where?"

They have made their point and it is a good one—that peace is better than war, love is better than hate, that clean air and water are better than foul, that man, in the long run, if he is to survive, must think not only of himself. It's a corny line to say, perhaps, but he must try to be, in many little ways, his brother's keeper.

A Strange Mountain Winter

It has been a strange year in the mountains. The hard, bright days of snapping cold have seldom come. Only three times so far has the thermometer fallen low—once, on Christmas Day, to fourteen, and once again to twenty, and again to twenty-five. It has been a winter of foggy warmth, with the thermometer hanging in the low sixties. The rains have been like the rains of summer—great downpours lasting hour after hour. In the wet woods men cutting locust posts have seen yellowjackets out, a strange thing for the time of year, and now and then a grasshopper leaps in the grass on dry days.

The creeks run full, like the creeks of spring, and beside the house, close by the tumbling stream, an old peach tree fooled by the warm rains and the balmy air, is beginning to swell its buds. There is not the look of life in the woods, where all stands gaunt and bare, but on a muggy morning there is the smell of life, a faint fragrance of bush and shrub.

The deer still move about—though not in such numbers now as in the bright autumn, when the hunting season was on and guns were hammering all over the mountains. They have not yet yarded up on the ridges, in the thickets, for the cold and cutting winds have not come. An hour ago, fifty yards from the house, a big buck walked calmly down to the shallows where the stream empties into the lake. He stood a moment and then walked through the shallow water and out on the other side, across the road and into the great meadows that stretches up the hill. He looked fat and sleek, as if forage was still to be found in plenty.

The muskrats are still busy at the little pond up the road, and you can see where they came out by moonlight to cut the cattails and the swamp grass with which, I suppose, they line their houses underneath the bank. There is no ice on the pond, and it is easy to see where their tails run in the mucky shallows, leading up under the banks of the ponds. The squirrels are also busy.

It has been a time of beautiful sunsets. Riding the mountain just at dusk the other evening, we saw the mountains wearing robes of gold never seen in the summertime. The haze of twilight on the hills is a dusty blue, and deeper shadows that lie in the folds of the hills are richly purple, and the sunsets are the crimson of a ripe apple highly polished, not the red and gold of summer.

In the house there is a deeper chill than in the balmy sun outside, and the feel of a fire is good. But there is no need for a leaping blaze. Only the simmer and steam of logs, sending off as much smoke as flame, keeps the room warm enough. But the smell of the burning hickory is as much a blessing as the little glowing heat the fire bestows. There is a nip in the air, if you sit without moving in a shady place, but even a short walk brings a warm glow and a sweater is a burden.

The balmy days are about over, though. Maybe this one is the last, the old-timers say who live here the year round. This morning there was a streak of strange, brownish clouds across the sky, high up, whipped out in ribbons and streamers. Behind these prophets of changing weather came a billowing mass of gray— dirty gray, like the inside of an old cotton-stuffed mattress broken open. That means snow, they say, and after the snow, as in years past, will come clear shining skies, and a glittering pure white world of crackling cold above and crunching cold underfoot.

It would be a fine thing to stay and see it, walking in the snow

by day, following the deer tracks and the rabbit tracks and the tracks of the fox and the possum and the coon.

But already the gals, with an eye on the sky, and the curtain of gray that blots out the sun, are scurrying around stowing things away, and gathering up the million odds and ends of gear to pack away in the car, and in a little while I must pour water on the burning fire and carry the wet ashes out, and the charred and steaming chunks. That saddens me, somehow, for with the dead fire goes all the warmth and the contentment, and the drowsy ease and peace of mind which folks find all too seldom, and which always, once they've found it, ends too soon.

Spring Weaves Its Cool Tapestry

Maybe it was the long hard winter, with its deep snow and sleet. Maybe it was the late wet spring, with the long days of fog and rain. Whatever the reason, the sun of May has turned the mountains into a tapestry of colors as bright and varied as autumn. The difference is that the colors of fall are hot colors—crimson and rich glowing browns. The colors of spring are cool colors—a million different shades of green, the golden-greens and gray-greens and silvery green of the young hardwood trees and the deep almost-black green of the pines.

And under this overlay of many-shaded green lies the white of the dogwood, scattered on the steep mountain slopes like old snow.

When the sun shines and the wind blows, the whole surface of the mountain shimmers with many colors, like an opal in firelight, and sometimes the great bulk of the hills looks like the surface of a sunlit sea.

It is a joy to walk in these spring-bright woods in the cool of the afternoon, for there is the smell of sweet-shrubs in them, and the smell of sunwarmed pine, and the nameless odors of a thousand different drifting pollens, the life-seeds of the forest.

Everything is astir in these woods—the chipmunks and the little brown mice and, when you stop to listen a moment, the buzz and hum of a billion unseen insects make a high thin singing. There are many little blue violets under foot, and tiny white and yellow flowers I cannot name, and even the old dead gray mosses have taken on subtle colors of pink and pearl and purplish blue.

The best part though is not to walk at all, but just to sit on the porch and look out across the open space to the rise of the mountain. For here many birds come and go.

First a catbird bobs by, and perches, making a noise like a kitten makes when you pull its tail, half angry, half plaintive. And tiny bluebirds fly past that are bluer than backyard bluebirds, and little yellow birds the color of sunlight. But the most spectacular of all are the scarlet tanagers, flashes of brilliant crimson with jet black wings, which swirl above the long meadow grass hunting insects.

Then when night comes on, the birds disappear, but the sound of their singing lingers, and from the thicket down by the creek comes the song of the wood thrush, which is the sweetest of all bird songs.

And the sparrows are singing, and all the little birds that do not sing, but just make cheeping, chirping, chipping noises are talking as they settle down for the night. As full dark comes on there is a moment of deep silence. Then the first star comes out, and the whippoorwills start, and the frogs down by the pond; and the wind rustles in a billion leaves, and it's time to sleep.

Gentle Lady Leaves
Her Beloved Garden

One of the sweetest, loveliest, gentlest ladies Atlanta ever knew received the other day the most precious gift a kindly Father can bestow upon His children when their work is done—the blessing of a quick and happy death. Kneeling in her garden at the old home up at the mountain, adding another touch of beauty there as she had done each spring for so many years, Mrs. Joseph Winship died of a heart attack, quickly, quietly and without pain. Around her as she slipped away was the beauty she had loved so long. Through the trees that rimmed her garden shimmered the lake which had brought her and her family here to the Georgia hills every summer for nearly thirty years. Around her rose the ancient mountains, their old, tortured storm-broken trees moving gently in the spring winds, the soft new green of their leaves shining in the April sun.

Around her also was all the beauty she herself had created, the masses of mountain shrubs and flowers—laurel and rhododendron and azaleas—that she had brought from lonely hillsides and planted here.

It had been a happy day for her. Early in the morning, with baskets of bulbs her friends had given her, she had driven from

85

Atlanta to spend the Easter holiday in the place she loved the best. It was to be a happy weekend. Over the highways from Atlanta and Chattanooga her family was gathering. Daughters and their husbands, with a multitude of young, were hurrying to reach the big house by the lake and the happiness that always awaited them when they went to visit "Mama Nell." The first who came found her there among the flowers, gay and as happy as they'd ever known her.

With Bingham, her ancient butler, cook and gardener, spading the rich black soil for her, she was planting bulbs, talking of all the things she wanted to do while the fine spring weather held.

It was only a little later that they heard Bingham call. When they reached her she lay as if asleep, her hand still holding the clump of weeds she was trying to tug away from the roots of a tiny flower.

Later Bingham remembered something she had told him long ago.

"When my time comes," she had said, "I hope I'll be right here digging in my garden."

It was a simple statement of desire. It was answered as a prayer.

I think she would be happy to know the job she started was finished.

After the funeral, Bingham, an old man, went back to the mountains alone to finish planting the flowers "Miss Nell" was planting when she died.

And all of us who knew her will be grateful that he did, for they will blossom there forever in memory of one who, as Dr. Pierce Harris said of her, knew the truth of the poet's words: "One is nearer God's heart in a garden than anywhere else on earth."

In an Unaccustomed Silence, a Little Symphony of Nature

Now is the hour of silence, the time when all the world is hushed, as if God had said softly to the spinning globe: "Peace—be still." Moments ago, in a glory of gold and crimson cloud, the sun disappeared below the rim of the farthest western hill. Shadows fill the valley, blue-purple in the dusk. There is a glow of light still in the sky, but no living thing stirs.

Across the meadow the great mass of the mountain, forever astir, forever whispering with the million voices of the leaves, is as still and silent now as a painted mountain.

No bird sings or flutters there. No leaf moves. The ever-wandering, ever-murmuring wind is still. From the eaves the little bronze wind bells, that long ago in a Japanese temple soothed the ghosts of the samurai with their faint music, hang motionless.

The human ear is not accustomed to such silence. The mind does not quickly adjust to it, for rarely in life, from the moment of our birth until the hour of our death, do we know such quietness. Only the stone-deaf live in this utterly noiseless world of death-like hush.

Then in the darkness on the mountainside there is a sound like a faint groan, a creaking sound of old dry dead wood fibres wrenching apart. There is a feathery rustle of leaves and a thump as a dead limb, killed years ago by ice and tearing winds, breaks away and falls.

This breaks the spell. In the meadow some little insect begins a thin high singing. A cricket starts his evening song—zeh, zeh, zeh —like a little saw, pauses a moment, and starts again.

A whippoorwill gives his throat-clearing cluck, and then fills the valley with his mournful quavery cry. A bat swirls by with a little squeaking sound.

Above my head there is a faint buzz like a dentist's tiny drill, and wood dust fine as powder falls on my arm. A carpenter wasp, deep in a ceiling plank, has gone back to his labors.

The still wind rises from its hiding place and begins its restless wandering, and all about, the trees begin to speak in low and sleepy murmurs. The little bronze temple bells begin their golden tinkling in answer to the wind. The last light fades from the sky, the deep dusk comes, the first star winks. An owl calls and the frogs begin their bass and tenor colloquy and the silent world is alive again.

Save the Baby—or Catch the Bass?

It is a strange sight when the urge to land a fish, which is a deep urge, comes into violent conflict with an even deeper instinct, such as mother love.

The other day a lady of my acquaintance was placidly fishing from the long, narrow wooden boat bridge at the lake when she observed her small daughter, aged two, come toddling out on the bridge, wobbling from one side to the other, and stopping now and then to peer over the side at her own reflection, teetering dangerously over ten feet of water into which, of course, she would have sunk like a stone.

And just as Mama sighted her child wobbling out on the bridge, a large, belligerent bass who had not heard that it is beneath the dignity of a bass to bite a red worm, struck with a tug and a wallop and set her line to singing on the reel. For the next three minutes or so, I guess she was about the busiest lady in the United States. She would reel in a little line and make a leap toward the approaching baby and stop to give the fish a little line and make another leap and then reel in some more. Then the baby, attracted by the commotion in the water, flopped down and started crawling toward the edge and Mama gave a tremendous yank and the bass came sailing through the air and landed on the bridge with a thump and she let it lie and dived for the baby, pulling it back to safety. Then the bass flopped, shaking the hook loose, and she turned the baby loose and dived for the bass and the baby crawled toward the edge again and she turned loose the bass and grabbed for the baby and the bass—well anyway, that went on for awhile until the bass, showing very poor judgment, flopped so close to the baby they were both within reach and she seized one back of the gills, this being the bass, and the other by the seat of the rompers, and clung on desperately until both stopped flopping around.

Then, looking a little bedraggled, she came away clutching them both and for a while she was so distraught about the whole matter I thought she was going to spank the bass and string the baby on a twig.

The Little Bass Learns From Papa

There is a bass here of character so noble I think I shall try to emulate him. He is the father of even more offspring than I am, some thirty-odd it looks like, though they are somewhat hard to count, they keep moving around so much, and he spends the whole day doing nothing but looking after their health and welfare. I don't know where his wife is. Probably at her bridge club, maybe, or the garden club, or maybe she has had a lot of shopping to do recently. Anyway she is not around and he has to take care of the children.

He is doing a wonderful job of it. He swims around them, keeping them herded together in a tight little cluster, and when one of them starts to swim off, over into the very shallow water where presumably a turtle might be lurking, he cuts in front of it and herds it back into the little tight-knit group. Now and then two or three, more adventurous than the rest, or more foolish perhaps, seem inclined to want to explore the deeper waters where all manner of dangers lurk, such as their uncles and aunts who presumably would be delighted to dine on a small nephew or niece. When this happens he goes into a tantrum, scooting this way and that until they are together again.

This afternoon he seems to be giving them a lesson in the wiles of fishermen and how to live to a ripe old age despite the dark plots of plug casters and worm fishermen. There must have been a dozen people who came out on the footbridge this afternoon to watch the big bass with his young. And every one of them has done his best to catch the old man. They have tantalized him with shiny plugs that skip along on top of the water like a jubilant minnow, and with plugs which emulate a small frog, and with plugs which dive for the bottom and scoot along there with such realism that even I, myself, thought it was a little silver-gray fish, even though I had just seen the man cast it.

He has investigated all three lures, coming up to them and looking them over, while the children clustered around looking on, and then, with a haughty look and something resembling a sneer on his countenance, he has swum off disdainfully. They have tried to tempt him with red worms, and with large black and yellow worms which look so succulent and tasty it is hard to see how a fish in his right mind would ignore them, but he does not even come up and nose about these. He just swims by, yawning slightly, as if bored, and it is plain to see that he is somewhat insulted that the fishermen should think he would be taken in by such a crude lure.

Now and then one of his fry, being foolhardy, will be attracted by the splash of the plug as it enters the water, and will rush over and follow along after it as if wanting to strike it, and when this happens the old man will dart in between him and the lure and send the little fellow packing back in a hurry. I think probably he gave him a few wallops with his tail but it is hard to see plainly just what goes on under four feet of water, even if it is fairly clear.

But when a stupid bream, or perch, or a big dumb minnow with more courage than brains came along to make a pass at a red worm, or a catawba, the old bass would make no move to warn him whatsoever. He would let him go on and get hooked and then he would swim slowly around the school, evidently saying to his own: "See, that's what I am trying to tell you. Now you pay attention to your father, for I know what I am talking about."

It is very interesting to stand for an hour or so watching the old

92

bass instruct his children. But it is somehow a little disturbing, too. For it makes me feel that I ought to be spending more time pointing out to my own the snares and delusions which they must avoid, and teaching them that some of the things which look most appealing actually conceal sharp barbed hooks which will hurt them.

It is a distressing thought when it occurs to a man that he, who is one of the Lord's noblest works, is not as good a father as a fish.

Ages of Man at Play

I trust that my friends of the young married set who are still in the baby-having business will not take offense at this, but the facts are that this place up here is beginning to look like a seal rookery.

Down at the dock in the mornings the babies are so thick under foot that a man is afraid to walk about for fear he will step on one, and the water around the dock is so full of them that trying to swim there is like trying to paddle about in a school of herring. They swim about as well as herring, too, spending as much time under the water as they do on top of it.

In fact, newcomers to the place have been known to come boiling out of the water, bug-eyed, under the delusion that the lake is infested by octopuses, for it is a favorite sport of some of the more amphibious small fry to swim down deep under some fat and elderly dog-paddler and give him a sharp pinch on the ham.

It makes a man feel his years to see all the kindergartners about, for it seems to me that it was only yesterday that the mamas and papas of these youngsters themselves were romping about in the water in bathing suits no wider across the seat than the span of a man's hand.

There are about four ages of young'uns around the place now.

94

There is the diaper set, a half-dozen or more round, fat ones, whose eyes do not focus yet. They lie around on blankets in shady spots under the trees, glugging away at their bottles, or snoozing, or just lying there waving their feet in the air.

There are about a dozen more of the next size larger. These are the baby pool set, who go in the water at the edge of the lake, and sit there, splashing, and happily lifting up handfuls of wet sand and rubbing it in their hair. When they get tired of doing this they go wandering around with little buckets full of muddy water, pouring it on the old folks, who are lying on the dock with their eyes shut, sunbathing.

This crowd, which is made up of about equal parts boys and girls, also like to waddle up and down the dock, picking up people's shoes, and sunglasses and sunburn lotion, and towels and cigarettes, and throwing them into the water.

There is a very active member of this set who is about half knee high to a grown man. He has blond curly hair and two front teeth, and a fat stomach which sticks out, and he wears a pair of baggy red trunks that hang down just above his ankles. He goes around among the old folks sitting on benches under the trees, pouring sandy water in their shoes, and when they leap and yell he laughs heartily and puts out his hand and says, "How do you do?" very politely.

There is an intermediate group who are too big for the baby pool, and too little to go in the deep part, who have to be watched all the time because they want to do what the older kids are doing, and are always getting out over their heads and going under, glub, glub, glub, causing great consternation on the dock until somebody fishes them out. They do not seem to be distressed at this, but go back out where it's deep again as soon as they find out nobody is looking.

This causes their parents a great deal of nervousness, of course, but their determination is a fine thing, for pretty soon they are out in the deep, swimming good as anybody else, and jumping off the twenty-foot tower and doing front flips off the spring board.

It is a fine thing, on a hot summer morning, to sit there, under the trees, watching the little ones tug at their bottles and coo, watching the others busy with their myriad enterprises.

A few years ago it began to look as if the race was growing old and tired. People just weren't having lots of babies any more. Now that's all changed. Maybe the past war caused it. Maybe the threat of future wars.

Whatever the reason, some deep instinct in the race is causing people to multiply and replenish the earth as the Book admonishes them to do. And I for one think it's a fine thing.

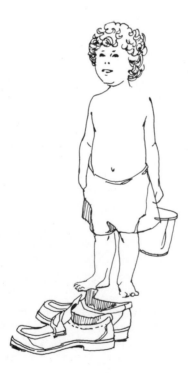

Strangers in the Mountains

Not long ago I reported the death, by fire, of one of the old big houses at the mountain. I use the word "death" advisedly, for when a house has been lived in as long as had the Wright house, by so many people who loved it so well, it does take on a personality, a life of its own.

There were three families who made their summer residence in the old house at the time of the fire—though none were there when lightning set the blaze—and such was the spell in which it held them, none were able to leave it and go elsewhere for the summer even though they had no roof over their heads. Instead, they bought and borrowed and begged and scrounged tents and sleeping bags and blankets and outdoor stoves and lanterns and deep in the thickets beside the lake they set up their camps, far enough from the road that they would be sheltered from prying eyes when they went down to the cove with a cake of soap for a skinny-dip bath, but not so far they could not walk to the edge of the copse and look up and see the green grass growing on the grave of the old house.

And here, through drouth and storm and fog and misty drizzle they passed the summer, growing leaner and browner and a little more tattered, earth-stained, shaggy and uncurried every day.

But on the whole, surviving blithely, doing a little painting and drawing by day, reading—and writing—a little poetry by night, tuning their lives to the rhythms of the hills and their many melodies, from the flute-song of the morning birds to the great drumrolls of midnight thunder.

Then came the night after the annual meeting, a time of gentle madness at the mountain when minnesingers and minstrels and troubadours wander in the darkness and toasts are drunk and songs are sung, and nobody, even the smallest child, gets to bed much before the dawn. And so it was in the Kiser camp in the midmorning after this great event, and I now let an in-law who was a witness take up the tale.

"It was just about the time the fog begins to lift from the lake," she said, "and Mimi, still groping woolily in her own personal fog brought on by the revels of the night before, rolled from a sleeping bag like a good mother should to put the coffee pot on the fire. It had just come to a boil and there were groans and stirring among the lumps that were her sleeping young, when all at once came hell's own popping noise and out of the lifting fog there swooped a crippled helicopter, its great vanes beating, to land with the gentlest of bumps and bounces on an old green of the golf course.

"The pilot, a neat young man with a worry wrinkle between his brows you could lay a pencil in, stepped out and his first impulse seemed to be to get back in again and take off at once even if his bird was crippled. For what he was seeing was like a scene from Tolkien, with Frodo and his hobbits tramping out of a misty glen to surround him—the hobbits of course being Kisers of all assorted ages, sexes and sizes, who had lunged from their sleeping bags at the first pop-pop of the sputtering motor. Peering tousled and agape from beneath great ricks of sleep-rumpled hair they surrounded the helicopter while their dogs, also of all assorted shapes, sizes and sexes, but running mainly to low-slung black

Scotties, circled in idiot frenzy beneath the still lazily turning blades.

"From the plane four passengers peered somewhat nervously, finally descending to deploy themselves in pairs, two being brisk young male lawyer types, two others lady realtors, dressed in white and high heels, the four of whom, it was learned later, having chartered the chopper to seek out recreational spots in this once lonesome heart of the hills.

"Mimi, as matriarch of the tribe, felt her obligation to offer the hospitality of the mountain, so she invited the droppers-in to have coffee. So they made their way then with the whole tribe of young Kisers trooping along, down a little path to the little clearing by the lake where the Kisers had set up tentkeeping with the salvaged stools and tables they had borrowed, or rescued from the ashes of the house. To the visitors it could only seem that they had dropped into some hidden and forgotten pocket of Appalachia where a lorn mother was valiantly bringing up her tribe of young under the most primitive of conditions. Their sympathy was obvious.

" 'The children,' said one of the lady realtors, tentatively, 'Do they read?'

"Mimi didn't blink. Rolling an imaginary snuffstick to the corner of her mouth, she nodded toward Howard her oldest son. 'Yes, maaa-um,' she said. 'This-un can read readin' real good. But he can't read ritin' yit.' "

The Lizard Does All the Work

I have been making a brief study of the human race here lately and I have come to the conclusion there are just three kinds of people in the world—people who go fishing and catch fish, people who go fishing and don't catch any fish but keep going fishing anyway, and people who have got too much sense to go fishing in the first place.

For a good many years now I have been a stubborn member of the nonfishing fraternity. The last fish I ever caught was a six-inch catfish, caught on a set-hook baited with beef liver, in the Hudson River in Banks County, in the summer of 1923. I didn't get to eat him. When I took him off the hook he finned me in the meaty part of the thumb, twirled his whiskers triumphantly and flopped back into the river.

At that time I made a stout resolution. If the fish would leave me alone, I would leave them alone. For nearly thirty years, I lived up to my part of the bargain. Last week, though, I weakened sadly, and have now, I fear, moved into that doggedly unhappy class of people—the ones who go fishing but never catch a fish.

For some reason I cannot quite explain, except by the fact that a man does foolish things in his early forties, I found myself sitting in a leaky rowboat in the middle of a lake, accompanied by two fishing zealots and a quart fruit jar containing a dozen surly-looking spring lizards.

I was, my companions told me, fixing to catch me a mess of fish. Ordinarily, they said, to catch fish a man only had to have a little more sense than the fish. If he was baiting with spring lizards, though, he didn't have to have any sense. All he had to do was drop the spring lizard in the water and give it time to seek out a big bass and dive down its throat with the hook.

That's what they said. And that's what they did. The one in the bow caught fish, and the one in the stern caught fish. I didn't catch any fish. On the first cast my lizard took off like a bird and landed in the top of a willow tree, wrapping the line around the limb. When I finally got him back in the water he was a little groggy, but he did his best.

Every once in a while a tingle would come along the line, indicating he had a bass hemmed up in a corner and was trying to hook him. Then I'd rear back on the line and start reeling in, hollering for somebody to get the net ready, I had a monster.

The only thing I pulled in was my lizard. He was all scarred up where he had forced his way down the bass's throat, scratching himself on his teeth, and he looked at me reprovingly, as if to say, "Well, Buster, whatta you want me to do? Wrap the line around his gills and swim back to the boat with him?"

For two days it went on that way. They'd cast by an old drowned log and catch bass and I'd cast by the same log and catch nothing. They'd cast in the marshy shallows and pull out a fish and I'd cast in the same shallows and pull back my lizard.

It was disheartening. But just wait. Those black spring lizards, I've been told, don't really know how to catch a bass. What you need is a red spring lizard. They outrun the fish, I understand, throw him down and hook him good and solid, and then ride him, leaping and thrashing, back to the boat. That's what I'm going to get me—some red spring lizards.

Sleeping in a Rowboat Has Some Dangers

Young fellow I know, named Davy Woodall, seems to me has hit on a method of communing with nature which his namesake, Davy Crockett, might have envied. Every night about the time the big white stars begin to wink and shine, he paddles out into the middle of the lake and goes to bed.

He's got him a broad-beamed rowboat, about the size of an old-fashioned bateau. There's just room enough in it for a short-legged canvas army cot, and a little field stove, and an old-fashioned crank-wound Victrola. He anchors his boat out in the middle of the lake, far enough out from shore so that young Martins and other rapscallions cannot hit him with a rock. Then he puts a nice soft melody on the Victrola, and crawls into the sack and lies there, watching the Big Dipper trudge across the sky, and the march of all the little winking stars, until he falls asleep.

In the morning he wakes up just about first light, and drops a line over the side and catches himself a little bass, or a bream or two. Then he lights a fire in his field stove and cooks his breakfast, while the Victrola grinds out a sprightly tune.

It's fine out there in the middle of the lake in the dark of the night, he says. There's so much looking and listening a man can do, if he's a mind to. The whole arch of the heavens is there to watch, and there's so much to hear. From the dark shorelines comes the cry of the owl, hunting mice, and the splash of the otters frolicking at the water's edge. The frogs are all singing in chorus, and you can tell, he says, where the otters are swimming, for when the frogs fall silent along a stretch of bank, you know the otters are there.

It's fine sleeping out in the middle, he says. There's always a little breeze blowing, enough to blow the mosquitoes away, and to rock the boat a little, making the water lap against the sides with a little chuckling sound. And every once in a while there is a thundering big splash when some old bass surges up to the top and wallops the water with his tail and goes down again.

It sounds like fine sleeping, and I might try it myself some night. But I don't know. I overheard a muttered conversation between two low characters, about twelve years old apiece, the other night, about how to sneak up on people sleeping in boats at night. Idea seemed to be that if you slipped an inner tube around your waist and paddled out right e-e-easy, you could slip up and grab hold of one side and give a big tug and dump whoever was sleeping in it, cot and all, into the water.

So I think I'll just stay where I am. If I want to see the stars, or hear the bullfrogs chunking, I can always stick my head out the window by my bed.

There Can't Be That Many Babies in the World

Someday, I guess, I'll get it straight in my mind, but right now it seems a little dreamlike. There just can't be that many babies in the world. One day there lay the lake as quiet as the canals of the moon, with nary a soul astir. Next day, the face of the earth was acrawl with young'uns. You waded knee-deep in them, to get to the water.

In the shade under the trees, baskets pink and blue held the little bitty ones, lying there in their underbritches, pawing at the air, trying to make their eyes focus on the sunbeams that twinkled through the leaves.

The sand pile was acrawl with them. Fat ones, not much bigger than some of the big bass that swim in the lake, they sat there solemnly scooping up handsful of sand and pouring it in their hair, or eating it, or poking at each other's noses with chubby exploring fingers. And once in a while, as if moved by some ancient urge to go back to the deep waters from which the scientists say all men have sprung, they would struggle to their all fours doughtily, and crawl, headlong, like small fat pink turtles, toward the lake. Then there would be a great scurrying of mamas, and a shouting, and they would be snatched from the edge of the waters and plunked, bellowing, back into the sand.

There was no room for them in the shallows anyway. There the next size bigger, the ones old enough to know you can't breathe under water, were at play. They clustered thick as a school of herring, lying on their tummies and splashing and yelling and bopping each other on the head with little tin watering cans.

It was a hard day for the mothers. They would lie there on the dock, in the warm sun, keeping a wary eye cocked to see that no small character went under and forgot to come up again, and the sun would anesthetize them and they would doze, and then wake with a look of panic and start counting heads frantically. Or bottoms, for under these circumstances a mama has to be able to recognize her offspring's derriere at a glance, for often that is the only part of him that is sticking out of the water.

It was a great day for grandmothers though. The matriarchs of the clans sat all day on the saggy old benches under the trees, holding damp sandy babies on their laps, happy as you please. Grandmothers do not get to hold babies nearly enough, this day and time, they tell me.

So it was a fine grand Fourth for everybody. Nobody got snake bit, and nobody got bee stung and nobody hit anybody else on the head with a small toy shovel hard enough to draw blood. And only one grandfather, who shall be nameless here, for he is a sensitive man, got in the doghouse. It was all his own fault though.

With a house full of babies on hand, he decided to see what caused the washing machine to squeak. So he took it apart.

He couldn't get it back together again. And the last I saw of him he was wandering the mountain, seeking a lodging for the night, afraid to go home and face the angry females of his family, and the mountain of diapers they swore they were going to make him wash.

105

The Screech Owl Sings the Tenor

The best time of day is that hour, just before darkness falls, when the sun sinks behind the shoulders of the big blue hills to the west, and the waters of the lake grow still, and the world is silent.

For a moment it seems that in all this quiet realm of sky and water there is no living thing. You can hear yourself breathe. You can hear the faint rustle of the leaves, though no breeze blows. You can hear the chuckle of the water, lapping at the bank, though no ripple moves on the surface of the lake. And you sit there in the boat, with your line dangling over the side, into the mirror-smooth water, and feel a great peace and a great loneliness and a vast sense of content.

And then all at once the spell is broken. A kingfisher flaps by with his strange bobbing flight and the sound of his harsh calling offends the silence. Somewhere, far off, a crow calls. In the shallows by the reeds a bug struggles on the water, and a little fish rises and swallows him, and the water boils for a moment with the violence of the lunge to the surface and the sudden downward turn, and the flap of the fish's tail on the water sounds loud in the silence.

Then all is still again, and in the shadows, under the alder bushes where they hang down low to the water, you see a silken movement. A dark triangular head appears and cleaves the water swiftly. An old snapping turtle, mean and hungry, is setting out on his nightly rounds of scavenging in the shallows for the little fish that died in the day's long struggle for survival.

And somewhere along the way he'll find the leg of a young rabbit, and thanking his turtle gods for this bounty, he'll clamp down his jaws upon it, and there will be a big hook in it, and the old turtle will end up in the soup. But now he is alive and swimming free, and you marvel at the speed with which so clumsy a creature glides through the water.

On the other side of the lake the last sun falls on a sleek and beautiful head. Some furry creature, a muskrat, or an otter, is making his way from his den deep in the bank, going out on his night's long prowl for food.

The first frog clears his throat, a little fellow who goes "kerrr-rink," "kerrrrink," "kerrrrink." And across the lake an old big frog chides him for his feeble note. The deep bass booms in the gathering dark like a cello—"korrrroooom," "korrrroom," "karrr-roooomp." And the frog chorus starts all around the lakeshore, mile after mile of great frogs and little frogs, singing their greeting to the coming night.

Then for no reason that a human being can understand, they all fall silent at once, as sometimes, at midnight, the whippoorwills suddenly stop singing, listening perhaps to a sound no human ear can hear.

And in the stillness, from the trees along the bank there rises a high, clear tremolo, a voice like the voice of all the friendly little ghosts who ever walked at night, a funny blending of quaver, and whistle, and plaintive sob—the voice of the screech owl, announcing to the universe that he is up and about and ready to do business.

Then all sounds blend together, cry of frog and owl, and splash of fish. The tuning up is over. The night's wild symphony has begun.

As the Stars Come Out
So Do the Fishermen

The first star comes while the western sky is still full of pink light. All of a sudden it is hanging there, flickering like a candle flame, rising so fast you can see it moving, climbing steadily up the sky.

With the coming of the star, the fishermen in the little boats take heart. All the long afternoon they have skirted the thick brushy banks of the lake, casting lures that are strangely and wondrously made, seeking to tempt the fish. They have offered them tiny, bright-colored flies that float so lightly they make no ripple on the mirror of the still water. They have offered them strange bug-shaped lures that skip along the surface, making a great commotion, like a distraught beetle that has fallen into the water and seeks to free himself.

They have dragged shiny bits of metal, adorned with yellow feathers, in the depths where the water is dark and cool—where the fat bass lie, the fishermen think, taking their ease in the heat of the long afternoon. They had offered lizards, fat and black and shiny, a toothsome morsel for a hungry fish. They have sat motionless for hours, dangling red worms over the bream beds. No fish.

But with the falling of the darkness and the rising of the star, life begins to stir on the margin of the lake and hope surges in the bosom of the fisherman. Up from the depths where they have lain all day, the bass come to the shallows to feed. Bugs wing, droning, over the cooling water, and all along the lake's edge the fish begin to break water, striking at the bugs. Everywhere, in the marshy shallows, in the deep places where the old dead trees lift their gaunt bare arms over the surface, under the hanging boughs of the alders and the willows at the water's edge, the fish are feeding noisily.

From the drifting boats comes the murmur of excited voices. The fishermen flog the waters, casting toward the splash and swirl where the fish are rising. Now and then a line snaps taut, a rod tip bends, and there is a flash of white and a thrashing as a small and foolish fish takes the hook and is brought alongside, struggling. But not often. And these are young fish, rash and impetuous. The old big fellows, the four and five-pounders are not deceived. They know, somehow, a bug from a plug, a juicy live insect from a man-made fly with a steel bar at its heart.

It is a good time to fish. It is a better time not to fish, but to lie back quietly in the drifting boat, and watch, and listen, to the life that is beginning to stir, in the air and on the banks and in the water. Against the deepening red of the sky a squadron of bats, like tiny dragons, swerve and dart in erratic flight. The evensong of the frogs begins. The deep cello notes roll like little thunder across the lake. Deep in his den beneath the banks the muskrat hears the voices of the frogs and comes out for his evening's hunting.

You can see him swimming there, in the shadows beneath the overhanging bushes, only his sleek black head showing, as he glides silent as a fish, toward the sound of the conversing frogs. Now and then, quietly as a shadow, he slides out on the bank, his chunky body dark and wet. Then the old frog, who has been bellowing so loud and boastfully, hushes suddenly, his deep voice breaking off in the middle of a deep "karoom." There is a flash and a splash as he leaps for the water, and down the bank, frustrated, the muskrat glides again.

In the last light you can see him, striking out across the lake toward the other side, and behind him soon the old frog, back on his podium of mud beside the water's edge, hurls insults after him.

"Go home, go home," he rumbles testily.

The evening star still climbs, alone in the western sky. To the east all is blackness now, and then many stars are out, but in the west where the last light lingers no star yet twinkles in competition with the great lamp hanging there. Off where all is dark, in the big trees back from the lake, a whippoorwill cries his sorrows to the world. Then he, too, falls silent and a new voice takes over. It seems to come from everywhere, and even the home-going fishermen stop to listen. It is the hunting cry of an owl, a shivery, ghostly call that floats and shimmers on the air, dying away as the last light fades. And now, the deep, black darkness falls, and the stars shine everywhere, and it is night at last. And the fisherman goes home, leaving the lake and its wonder and its mystery to frog and fish and bat and owl, to hunter and to hunted.

Something Special on the Fourth

This year somebody had the idea that maybe it would be nice to do something special on the Fourth of July—not only the fireworks at night, which we always had, very exciting, and very beautiful, with the black sky over the lake all ablaze with the gold and green and white and crimson clusters and showers of fire from the exploding rockets—but something in the daytime, too, with flags and music and people marching.

Nobody said this in so many words but the feeling seemed to be that the time had come to reaffirm in some tangible way a faith in the old values that in recent years had been so severely under attack, our loyalty to old credos that were once unquestioned, a belief in the America we once believed in, and in its democratic form of government as the last best hope of earth and in the flag in which all these things were symbolized.

So, we had a parade. And looking at it in one way, it was a pitiful, homemade thing. But looking at it in another, it was glorious. There were about sixty people in the line of march, I guess, the total holiday population of the mountain. It moved for a mile, along the dirt road that curved around the lake, and everybody in it either carried an American flag, or wore somewhere on his person a touch of the red, white and blue. Some of the

111

younger kids, and some of the teenagers too, even had star span-gled and red, white and blue striped shirts and pants on, but no-body seemed to feel that this was a desecration. For the mood of the people marching, though gay and happy, was not flippant. It was a mood of pride, and of love and affection, unabashed and unashamed, for Old Glory and all it stood for.

There was no Grand Marshal for this parade. It organized it-self. A little blonde fellow led it, riding one of those little putt-putt motor scooters. He had a big flag fastened to the scooter, and there was a strong wind blowing across the lake which made the flag stand out, pushed by the wind, billowing proudly. Behind him came the musicians, three young men, like that famous painting, with flag and fife and trumpet and the most battered snare drum this side of the Salvation Army, playing brave and glorious marching music. After the music came the mounted unit, seven little girls, as I remember, riding bareback on horses that snorted and bobbed their heads and pranced to the music, their manes and tails entwined with red, white and blue ribbon.

And behind the cavalry came the only float in the parade, a wheelbarrow, gaily bedecked, pushed by a gentleman with a black beard and occupied by a maiden of almost stunning beauty, wearing a circlet of black-eyed susans in her hair, and a virginal white T-shirt like a Greek toga. She represented the God-dess of Liberty.

Behind her came the marching units, a tatterdemalion crew in everything from granny glasses and granny skirts to hot pants and Bikinis, the males maned like lions, in bellbottoms or bathing trunks. But all, somewhere upon their person, had some bit of bunting, and all marched bravely to fife and drum. Bringing up the rear was a car or two, gayly decorated, bearing ladies too preg-nant to march a mile in the hot sun over a rough and rocky road, and a couple of lap children too small to walk at all. And running ahead and behind and around it all, with bunting in their collars and barking their heads off, there must have been a dozen dogs.

So moved the great parade at Burnt Mountain on American Independence Day. And right in the middle of it, something happened that seemed to have come out of some movie director's dream—though it was in no way planned. Halfway around the lake there stands, in the grove of trees between the road and the water's edge, the little white clapboard Burnt Mountain Church, a stronghold of the Baptist faith in these parts for nearly a hundred years. And as we came around the bend in the road, fife and drum fell silent, and all the marching people hushed their chatter. For there at the edge of the lake stood fifty-odd men and women, the entire congregation of Burnt Mountain Church, their backs to the road, their faces turned to the water. There, in the waist-deep water, stood the preachers who had conducted the revival meeting just ended at the church. And in the ancient ritual of baptism by immersion they were lowering down into the water and bringing straightway up out of the water, as John did our Lord in Jordan, the converts who had been saved during the week of revival.

We went past in embarrassed silence, with only the putt-putt of the scooters and the clack of the horses' hooves on the stony road to break the stillness. And once, from beyond the ranks of the watching people, we heard the happy shout of a man being baptized as he came up out of the water—"Praise the Lord."

A flag, flaunted by the wind, frightened a horse as we were passing and he snorted and lunged and there was a quick commotion. But the people of the congregation, with superhuman self-control, kept their eyes on the lake and the ancient sacrament being enacted there, never once turning their heads to see what in heaven's name was passing on the road behind them.

We went quietly on, across the dam and on to the grove by the swimming dock, where the musicians took their place on a high place above the road and played, as best it can be played with fife and trumpet and a broken drum, the Star Spangled Banner. And that was a great moment and the fireworks display that night was more spectacular than ever. But the high point of the day to many of us came in those few moments when, completely by accident, two profound components of the American dream came into brief juxtaposition—the little parade, with its meaning of

113

faith in country and flag, and the baptism at the little country church, with its meaning of faith in God and His Son, unchanged and unchanging down the years.

All Family Rows Forgotten

All week in Washington in the steaming heat I kept thinking how nice it would be to get back down here where the cool winds blow. Well, the cool winds are blowing all right, bringing with them fog as thick as wood smoke that drifts in the windows and swirls through the room. And the wet wood in the fireplace steams and simmers and will not flame, for on these raw wet days of vagrant, shifting winds the chimney does not draw but pours its smoke into the room.

And outside, out of the fog the slow, sad rain is falling steadily, beating on the leaves, and no birds sing in the trees and the woods are silent. For all the little creatures that stir about on sunny days now are tucked away in hidden places, waiting out the weather.

But humans lack the calmness and the wisdom of wild things and they cannot live tranquilly together in their burrows on rainy days. So the house is full of spats and quarrelings and restless fretfulness.

They try, I'll admit, to amuse themselves. But the one who is trying to play the guitar and sing keeps hitting a sour note when he shifts from F to G. And the others yell at him to shut up, for gosh sakes. So, wounded, he puts the guitar down and puts a record on the record player, a bouncing rock-and-roll. And they start to dance to this music.

But the one over in the corner, painting designs on copper with powdered glass and baking it in a little electric kiln, starts bellowing a loud protest. For the house is old and shaky and the dancing makes the whole place tremble and she cannot paint the little wiggly lines with a sure hand while they are dancing.

So this starts another fight and I am just on the verge of getting up and laying about me with a stick, driving them all out in the rain, when the gray cat saves us all. Bored beyond all comprehending, the cat stalks in and sees the dog asleep and walks over and bats him across the nose. And up he rises in anguish and surprise and takes out after the cat and "Wham" she hits the screened door and plows through, with his teeth gnashing inches behind her fuzzed-up tail. Across the yard she flees, with the dog bellowing after, and up the wet bole of the big oak she scrambles, with the whole family yelling in pursuit.

And now all family rows are forgotten in the great overweening problem of how to get the cat down out of the tree. But the cat solves this too. For the wet dead limb where she crouches is slippery and as she shifts about she slips and falls. And everybody leaps to avoid the falling cat, for catching a falling cat is about like catching a roll of barbed wire. Except one small and valiant character, who does not leap aside. Like an end receiving a forward pass, he cradles his arms and catches the cat, unhurt, as she tumbles forty feet through the air.

And the fire steams and will not burn and fog swirls through the windows and the rain falls. But peace lies on the household now, for the day's grim gray grip of monotony and boredom for a moment has been broken.

When Rains Come, Do Birds Stay Dry?

You wonder about things sometimes. Like what happens to the little creatures in the woods when it rains. Half an hour ago the skies were clear and blue. Birds flickered through the woods beside the house, their wings glinting bright in the sun. Now the rain is here.

It came walking across the mountains from the flat lands beyond the hill. It brought life to the great massed bulk of the still mountain, sound that was first a whisper, then a shout as a billion raindrops struck a billion leaves and twigs. The color of the mountain changed with the rain, deepened and darkened as the rain washed the leaves clean of dust and pollen. It came across the valley like a moving wall of silver; the first few pattering outriders reached the house, drummed like fingers on the roof. Then like a cavalry charge, with a roar and a pushing of wind, it hit the house. (It came in the house, as a matter of fact, and there was a great running, and hollering of female voices, and the clatter of pans and double boilers and casseroles and whatever, being placed under leaks. Which is another thing that puzzles me. Sometimes when it rains the house is as dry and snug as can be, and again it leaks like a colander.)

But I drifted off the subject, which was, where do the birds go when it rains? Do they just sit on a limb in the wet woods, while the hard drops pound them? And what about the little creatures that live in the ground, the field mice and the chipmunks and the ground-nesting birds, like the quail and the whippoorwill? Do little freshets ever drown them or wash their eggs away? And what about the little birds that are newborn in their nests in the trees? Do they get cold when the cold rain beats on them—for these mountain rains are icy rains, even in summertime—and suffer from the sneezes?

And where do the bugs and beetles go? Do the rains pour down into their holes in the ground and drown them? And what about the deer and the coons and the rabbits? How do they stay dry? Or do they? And all the cat family, the wildcats and the bobcats. Do they, like house cats, hate to be wet?

It's nothing to worry about, I guess, for always, after a rain, in the soft earth beside the road, you see the tracks of all the wild things, mice and deer and rabbits, marked in the mud, as if they were frolicking about. And right now, with the rain gone, the clouds gone, and the late sun shining, the birds are out again. All through the woods you can see the flicker of their wings. Looks like, from here, they're dry as a bone. I can't understand it.

No One Will Believe This

The sky was high and blue and cloudless and the lake was deep green and clear, like a dark emerald, and a little wind was ruffling it just enough to make it ripple.

It was a fine day for fishing and as I hung the little electric motor on the stern and hitched it up to the battery, I felt that good feeling that a fisherman always feels—buoyant confidence that down there somewhere beneath the gently rippling water there is a bass as big as a young mule, just waiting for whatever shining thing with hooks on it you want to throw in for his pleasure.

So, not to waste a minute, we put on shiny spinners that would go down deep and set out, trolling across the lake to the quiet cove where the big bass are supposed to lie in the shallows, hunting for little fish.

But watching a rod and running a boat is too much for a man when he's out in a boat for the first time in the spring. His mind wanders to the high sky, where a jet plane, so high it was out of sight and soundless, was drawing a white chalk mark across the deep blue. And he sees a flicker of wings in the brush on the farther shore, where a kingfisher is hunting little minnows close to shore.

119

And in the path of the sun on the water, a muskrat swims, his black head wet and sleek, headed for the high bank where he makes his den. And on a dead pine a stub-tailed hawk sits like a king, peering down in the water with royal contempt for all that moved on it.

So, watching these things, I didn't notice I was letting the stern kick around until I heard Mama yell, and she horsed back on her rod, thinking she had a big one on. But what had happened was I'd let the boat swing and the propeller had caught her line and was wrapping it around the shaft at a very high rate of speed.

So we stop and drift, and for about an hour we unwind the line from the propeller shaft, and by the time we get the line clear we have drifted close to shore, and I put on an old beat up Lazy Ike, which has been dragged over so many logs its hooks are dull. And all of a sudden I feel the Ike hit something solid, and I think for a moment I have hung on a log again.

But a log does not all of a sudden rush about forty feet in one direction and then about fifty feet back again. And all at once there is a swirl of water out at the end of the taut line, and the biggest bass I ever saw explodes straight up in the air like a Polaris missile fired from under the sea.

He has a mouth that is wide as a bushel basket, and his tail is as broad as a man's two hands, and he has a hump on his back like a buffalo, and a great white sagging belly, and when he falls back in the water he makes a splash like a falling bomb.

He pulls like a horse, but I know he can't last long for when he jumps I see no sign of the Lazy Ike, with its savage hooks, hanging on his lip. He has swallowed it, deep down, and a fish that has hooked himself in such a way cannot fight long.

So I keep a tight line and crank him in and get him to about ten feet of the side of the boat and then—nothing—I am sitting there with the rod in my hand with about three feet of broken line hanging down from the tip like a spider web. And down in the deep dark-green water the granddaddy of all bass is swimming away to die somewhere with the hook in his belly.

It makes me so sad I just crank up and head for the shore and pull the boat out and go home and sit on the porch all afternoon, peering out at nothing, seeing in my mind's eye that big fish jumping out of the water, and knowing that nobody will ever believe me when I tell them how big it was.

Here in the Hills the Troubles of the World Seem Far Away

Over the years, as the young men have gone away to wars, or to travel, they have found brides in foreign countries, and have brought them back. So the place has taken on, slowly, a mild international flavor, a faint semblance of a cosmopolitan watering place, set in the frame of the Georgia hills.

Down on the dock in the afternoon you will hear a mother speak to her young in Spanish, and they will answer her back in their own strangely beautiful children's language, a mixture of mushmouth Southern English, and Castilian, and the Peruvian Indian patois that their nursemaid speaks. And a little further along you will hear another mother, singing to her baby a cradle song in German.

And along and along, visitors come from far places—an exchange student from Dusseldorf, tall and blonde, or a slim, dark British doctor.

You'd think, off hand, that this blending of the nationalities would give those of us who live here a greater awareness of the world and its problems and of what goes on elsewhere. But I am mildly sorry to report that this is not the case.

We try to worry about what's happening in Guatemala, and

what Mr. Dulles accomplished at Geneva, if anything. But it's hard to keep the mind focused on such matters. It's easier just to sit, watching the slow and stately wheeling of a big hawk, soaring over the meadows, hunting mice.

The matters the headlines howl of seem less important, actually, than the fact that a small boy with a well-flung stone has killed a rattlesnake on the road above the lake. Indochina, we comprehend, is a threat to the peace of all the world, and therefore a danger to us all. But the rattler, who had eight rattles and a button on his tail, was a near and ever-present immediate danger.

We try to become absorbed in the bigger things of course, for nobody can withdraw from the world. But the noises the statesmen make sound faintly here, and just at the moment we are straining our ears to catch the sound of their voices, somebody comes along and says that he saw a doe and her fawn, standing in the reeds by the old frog pond. And whatever vital matter we were pondering at the moment is forgotten.

But if the strangers who have come to us from afar have not been able to stir our sluggush intellects, they have helped us, and we them, perhaps, in other ways. Our children are picking up, I think, a little of the gracious courtesy, the shining politeness that is their heritage. And from us they are learning the easy, informal friendliness of the American. And each from the other, subconsciously, is absorbing an idea good for all men to know—that there are no great differences in people, whatever their nationality.

I think sometimes we puzzle them, though, by our habit of kidding, gently, those people we are fond of. And we have had to learn to keep our humor under control, for all we say, they take, at first, as truth. There was, for example, the distinguished gentleman from Austria, a whitehaired man, well aged, of corpulence and great dignity. Soon after his arrival here his son-in-law, in a moment of jest, told him that he could never be accepted as a fullfledged member of the colony until he had jumped from the diving tower. So he rose, and squared his shoulders as if he were about to face a firing squad and climbed the high ladder to the top, and with a look on his face like a man marching to certain doom, he strode to the edge and stepped off into space, falling thirty feet through empty air to land with a splash that set tidal waves to splashing against the further shore.

And nobody has had the courage to tell him yet, that it was all a rib—that the elders of the tribe never have jumped off the top tower in their lives, nor would they for a hundred dollars.

And there was the young Englishman in the canoe, dressed in his best trousers and shirt, with his camera slung about his neck, who sat, all unconscious, while his host, in a bathing suit, maneuvered the canoe below the tower and down from the tower suddenly plummeted a half dozen small boys, doubled up, who landed like cannon balls alongside the canoe, setting it awash and well-nigh drowning its occupants. Just a quaint old custom of the place, the host explained.

"Extr'ord'nry," the visitor said, stepping from the canoe, his flannels soaked to the knees, "but rather violent, don't you think?"

But the incident that lingers in the memory involves the gay, gallant, but credulous, young man from South America. He was told by a friend, solemnly, that it was a custom here, upon meeting a lady on the dock for the first time, to toss her overboard. Nobody paid much attention to such a palpable piece of foolishness. But the visitor, anxious to do the proper thing, stowed it away in his memory. And the next day, upon being presented to a young lady, he bowed from the waist, murmuring his pleasure in Spanish, straightened up, grabbed her by the scruff of her neck and the seat of the bathing suit, and tossed her, tail over teakettle, into the lake.

People Need a Hound Around

Somewhere, up in the hills back of my house, there's an old hound dog with a litter of pups, and I wish she'd get over her wildness, and her fear, and come on down here where folks can feed her, and look after her. But she's wild as a fox, as a deer, and nobody can get close to her.

I heard her long before I saw her. Night after night, over on the slope across the valley, or up on the high ridge back of the house, I've heard her running, chasing rabbits. But she never came near. Until late the other afternoon, just before good dark. I was sitting on the porch, looking out across the valley, thinking of nothing much, when I saw her coming down the hill.

She was moving along at an easy trot, a gaunt framework of skin and bones, and every once in a while she'd stop and sniff the wind. But she kept coming on, until she got about one hundred feet away. Then I made a mistake. I whistled at her. She heard the whistle, but she didn't know where it came from. And her ears went up and her big paws plowed the dust as she stopped and looked, and sniffed. Then she saw me, and it was funny, and pitiful, too. She fell a-sprawl as she tried to turn, her long legs thrashing. And then she got up and began to run. She didn't yelp or howl. She just took off in a shower of flying gravel.

125

I've seen her since, but not by day. Sometimes in the night my dog Shim will rouse and growl, and I'll wake and look out the window and see her—out by the scuppernong vine, or up by where the old barn used to stand. She's watching the house, remembering, I guess, long ago when somebody fed her, and scratched behind her ears, and gave her a place to sleep at night, out of the wet and cold.

But she won't come close. And when I whistle at her, she turns and goes, silent as a spotted ghost, back into the woods again.

We started putting out scraps for her, but she left them alone, her fear, I guess, being greater than her hunger, even though she is the hungriest-looking dog I ever saw.

The other night I thought I had her. Out where we'd left the scraps, I heard a rustling sound. Then Shim barked, and there came an answering bark, a queer half angry, half pleading, whine. So I got the flashlight and went out. But it wasn't the old lady. It was one of her pups, I guess, a tiny, gaunt, black and tan bag of bones, with big gray ticks hanging on his ears. He wouldn't run. When I'd move close he'd cower and whine, but when I'd reach out a hand to touch him he'd snarl and show his teeth.

So I left him alone. But maybe, before long, he'll gentle down, and get over his fear and wildness, and he and his old lady will become tame again. It's against the nature of the hound to run wild in the hills. Hound dogs need people around them. Just like, back where I come from, people always needed a few hound dogs around.

Uncle Jeems Was a Fine Shot

They say that Uncle Jeems, in the years of his great age, used to sit in a split-bottom chair outside the door of his log cabin—the old, old house that used to sit in the back yard after the big house was built—and shoot at the lock on the ginhouse door. He was using an old long rifle, of the type, I suppose, that Daniel Boone and Davy Crockett used. It was a muzzle-loading rifle and Uncle Jeems would load it very carefully.

He would take his powder horn, made of the horn of a steer, and pour a charge of powder into the little hollowed tip of deer horn that held exactly one charge. He would pour the powder down the barrel of the old muzzle-loader, and then carefully pick out a round ball he had molded himself, in the old bullet mold at night in front of the fire. And he would take a patch of soft cloth and place it over the muzzle, and on this patch he would place the ball, thrusting down the ball and patch with his thumb until it was level with the muzzle.

Then with a sharp knife—Uncle Jeems always kept his knife sharp—he would cut the patch off level with the muzzle. And then he would ram the patch and ball down snug against the powder. Then, on the little nipple with the pinhole in it that led to the powder chamber, he would place a cap. And then he would raise the rifle very carefully and draw a fine bead and "blip" he would shoot the lock on the ginhouse door and make it swing. He was a fine shot, they say, and it was very rare that he missed the lock.

After Uncle Jeems had spent most of the morning shooting at the lock on his ginhouse door he would rise and place his rifle on the rack above the doorway of his cabin and then you would see him walk out across the sandy yard, through the field and into the woods beyond. He would walk about a mile, a tiny, old-fashioned man, and he would go to the old Poplar Spring, deep in the woods, and kneel down and drink deep of the water. Then he would walk back to the house, taking it slow and easy, and take his rifle down from the rack above the door, and spend the rest of the afternoon shooting at the lock on the ginhouse door.

When they used to tell me about Uncle Jeems, sitting there all day, day after day, shooting at the lock on the ginhouse door, I used to think that Uncle Jeems was crazy, busying himself with such a pastime.

Now, I don't know. If he was crazy it may be that he passed on some of his craziness to his collateral descendants. A brother-in-law of mine loaned me a fine rifle with a telescope sight on it, and for two days now, from morning until evening, I have spent my time emulating Uncle Jeems. I am supposed to be out prowling the woods, trying to get a shot at that hawk, but that is too much trouble. It is better just to sit on the front porch, in a rocking chair, resting the rifle on the rail of the porch, shooting at a spot about the size of a half dollar—a bull's eye marked in lipstick on a sheet of white typewriter paper that I have set on the side of a sassafras bush down across the meadow.

Sometimes I hit the spot four times out of five, and sometimes just three times out of five and sometimes not that often. But always the bullets mark a pattern that could be covered with a baby's hand. This is very fine shooting, of course, for the spot is eighty yards away, but it is due to no prowess of mine that I hit it as often as I do. It is because the rifle, with its telescope sight, is a very fine precision instrument. All you have to do is set the little cross hairs on the bullseye, and squuuueeeeze the trigger gently, without blinking or flinching, and that's all there is to it.

Of course, you have to chase the cat off the porch, so he won't shake the floor by walking around while you are bringing the cross hairs on the bead, and you have to hold your breath so your breathing won't throw you off, and you have to fire sort of between heartbeats, as it were, because even the beat of your heart can throw you off a fraction.

And every time I fire a clip of five and go down and take a look at the pattern, clustered close around the bull's-eye, I feel pretty good. Until I think about Uncle Jeems and then I don't feel so proud. From what I've heard he shot just as well, using homemade bullets and an open sight. So far as I knew he never worried about holding his breath or his heartbeat. All he had to worry about was keeping his whiskers out of the way so a spark from the cap wouldn't set them on fire.

And I imagine if Uncle Jeems had had a rifle like this, with a telescope sight on it, he wouldn't have spent the day shooting at the lock on the ginhouse door. There wouldn't have been any sport in that. He would have plunked one bullet after another right through the key hole.

News Has a Flavor
in the Georgia Hills

Doc Roper came by last night, bringing the news of the mountain. Seems like everything's going on about as usual. Jezebel, the Allais' dog, got bitten on the nose by a copperhead. Made her head swell up as big as a dollar watermelon.

They took her down to Jasper and got her some shots that cost $12. That fixed her up all right, and pretty soon her head had shrunk until it wasn't bigger than a 25-cent watermelon. So they brought her home, and she jumped out of the car and ran over to the same patch of bushes and started snuffling around, and pretty soon "Bam" the same copperhead hit her again in the same place, just about, and her head started to swell up again.

So they took her down to Jasper and got more shots, costing $12. Which makes $25 that the Allais have got invested in Jezebel, which makes her about the most expensive dog on the mountain.

Finally, it occured to somebody that it might be a good idea to kill the copperhead before it ate Jezebel plum up. So Oley, who drives the truck with the mowing machine blade on it, came along and started mowing down the bushes where the copperhead made his residence.

He didn't have to wait long. Pretty soon there was a squirming and flopping in the bushes, and there lay the old copperhead, sliced into three parts pretty as you please.

Doc Roper says that there aren't as many reptiles around this year as usual. He thinks it's because there has been so much wet weather. He thinks that rattlers and other low venomous characters don't move around so much when it's cool and damp.

It's been a fine year for the trees though. He said he'd never seen the like, the way the trees have put on new growth this summer. In last year's drouth they were thin of leaf and scraggly-looking, but this year they have made up for it. He said he'd bet that if you cut a tree next year, this year's growth ring would be as wide as a man's thumb.

He says you can examine the rings and find out what the weather was like in any given year in the past, for as far back as the tree was alive. He says if you had a tree that was old enough, say 200 or 300 years old, you could examine the growth rings and figure out the cycles of the weather, the alternating years of rain and drouth, and project into the future, so you could pretty well tell whether the summer of the year 2000 was going to be dry or wet.

Doc knows a lot about the woods and the mountains, for he is a third-generation mountain man. His grandfather used to raise sheep on these hills.

He said his grandfather was a little bitty man about five feet three inches high. He had flaming red hair and red whiskers and, though he didn't weigh but 128 pounds, he wouldn't take anything off of nobody, not even a sheep.

Doc said his grandfather once bought a fine ram to improve his flock with, and brought him home to Pickens County. Doc's grandpa had a big old rambling house with a big piazza on it and he kept his firewood in one corner of the piazza.

One night he went out in his nightshirt to get a log to put on the fire. As he bent over to pick up the log the old ram who was sleeping over on the other end of the porch saw Doc's grandpa bent over the woodpile.

He got a running start across the porch and hit Doc's grandpa squarely in the seat of the nightshirt. He knocked Doc's grandpa clean over the bannister and into a big brambly rambler rosebush. Doc said his grandpa sailed through the air with a log of wood still in his arms. He sat there in the rosebush, hollering for his wife.

"Lou," he hollered, "what was that?"

"Why Paw," she said, "that was old Roebuck. He butted you."

"Well," said Doc's grandpa, climbing out of the rosebush, "me or him one has got to leave here."

So Doc's grandpa got up early the next morning and got him a pitchfork and took out after his prize ram, and ran him all the way into Cherokee County.

133

Music Reflected Moods of the Lake

After supper everybody on the mountain gathered up their young'uns and their dogs and loaded them in the car and piled folding chairs in on top of them and drove over to the Dobbs house to see the play. They lined the chairs up on the gravel in the turnaround, facing the garage, where somebody had painted one lone piece of scenery—a backdrop of mountains stretching away into the distance, the way the mountains look from the ridge above the lake.

It was cool there in the dark night, with a Greek chorus of crickets singing and dogs of all shapes and sizes walking about among the people, visiting with each other and getting acquainted.

Nobody expected to hear or see anything memorable or exciting. It was a homemade play and it would be interesting, all right, for people's kids were in it and maybe their wives. But fine exciting plays just don't get written and performed by amateurs in people's backyards in the mountains.

But sometimes, maybe, they do.

For when Joe Cumming, who wrote the play and the music too, started thumping on the old piano, which was all the music we had, and the chorus started singing, people suddenly fell very quiet and shushed their babies and their dogs and listened. For here was something good and real. ... Summertime in the mountains, the sun bright and the winds cool and the smell of a thousand flowers and pollens and the hum of bugs and the frogs chunking and the laughter of children playing in the lake.

It was all in the music—the moods of the lake at different hours of the day, from misty morning through brass-bright noon to soft plush night sprinkled with stars. It was all there—the quiet excitement of coming up for the first time with the car loaded and the kids keyed up and the dreamy drowsy middle days when a picnic is a great adventure and finally the quick last days so soon gone by.

Then the good sweet song—minor keyed, saying "goodby to summer," and the last one, "Hurry Now to the World Below," to the workaday world of jobs and school with summer and the mountains and the lake just a gentle, glowing memory.

It was beautiful and meaningful not only to one little isolated group who share their summers together but to anybody anywhere who ever knew and felt the magic of summer's spell.

And I wish I were smart enough to write the book for a bright and gay and happy musical, for with Joe's melodies as its core it would be wonderful!

The Night Has Its Own Song

It was a fine, fair day, the kind a dry fall brings to the mountains, with the leaves just beginning to show the first faint trace of color, and a high clear sky, with a drift of slow-moving clouds in it, far up, and on the ground a wind blowing with the faintest breath of winter. It was a good day for an amateur nature-lover, who might not know the habits of the wild things which live in the woods, but who loves to see the stir and bustle that goes on in the hills, as all growing and living things prepare for their long winter sleep.

First there were the fish. It was as if they missed the people who had swum there all summer, and who were taking one last swim in the chilling water, that had turned from its summer's murky blue to the clear amber of iced tea, or an old sherry long in the cask.

Ignoring the hopeful fishermen, drifting in the coves, luring them with fat worms, they clustered around the ladder at the swimming dock, and when a panting swimmer paused there they came in schools and nipped at him.

There were little fellows—chunky bream with black spots at the base of their dorsal fins, their translucent tails a shimmering green in the tawny water, and little bass, slim as your finger, with the black markings just beginning to show on their backs. We fed them stale bread, and they came by hundreds to snap at the bread as it floated on top of the water.

Then, in a flash, they were gone, and down below, so far the sun's lost light could hardly penetrate, we saw the thing that had put them to flight. It was a big old bass—shaped like a submarine, a dark shadow, thick in the shoulders, and as long as a man's arm from wrist to elbow. He had come to see what all the flurry was about. But he disdained the bread as he had disdained all the gaudy lures that had been tossed into the waters where he lay. Which is why, no doubt, he is a big old bass, still swimming free, and not stuffed and hung on a varnished plank over somebody's mantelpiece.

We left the fish and drove on around the lake, along the little dirt road to the house. And all at once, in front of the car, loping along easy and slow, across the road there moved a stranger not seen before. He was twice as big as the biggest tom cat, and there was something catlike about him, but not domestic cat. Short of body, long of leg, round of head, dark of coat, with a tail neither stubby nor long that hung in a curve like the tail of a lion in a zoo, he moved, with neither fright nor arrogance, across the road and into the woods.

It was, we learned later, what the mountain folk call a catamount, a wildcat's cousin. A bigger, bolder animal, and one not seen in the hills in the memory of the oldest men. And they told us to listen at night for his wild cry. For a catamount's cry is said to cause the skin on the scalp to crawl, and the marrow in the bones to turn to water.

So we sat on the porch in the dusk, as night came on. And we heard the singing of the night begin. The thin, high, steady droning that never rises or falls and never ceases, the song of a million little insects, singing in the trees. And over this undertone of singing sounded the busy cry of the crickets. And the whir of a chimney sweep's wings in the dark, and now and then the angry chirp, like a harsh bird call, of a chipmunk upset about something. But no catamount ever squalled.

Nor did any other strange sound break the night until late, when the fire was dying low and the smell of the smoke was in the room, more sedative than any sleeping tablet. Then out of the dark came a squealing shriek, quickly shut off, and close upon it the wild, eerie, harrowing cry of a big owl, laughing his ghostly laugh at having caught some small night-ranging mouse.

And that was all.

But I hope next time that catamount, from a good safe distance away, will look down on the sleeping house, and smell the wood smoke, and the strange and fearful scent of human beings, and sound off one good hair-lifting cry. Just so I can know what great-great-grandpa felt like, long ago, when he lay in his bed and listened to the wild voices of the night.

The Indians Can't Come Home

We found the arrowhead in the mud of the claybank beside the little stream, where the heavy rain had washed it into view. I picked it up and looked at it and handed it to the little boy and he looked at it, puzzled.

"Why did the Indian leave it here?" he asked. "Did he lie down and die and leave it here?"

"Maybe he lost it," I said. "Maybe early in the morning he came down through the woods, looking for a deer, and right here the deer was standing, maybe bending his head to drink. And the Indian slipped up close to shoot. But when he shot, maybe a little twig or something was in the way and it made the arrow go crooked. And he missed the deer and it ran away."

"Then did the Indian lie down and die because he missed the deer?"

"No," I said. "That didn't make him die, for he had other things to eat beside the deer. He had berries and nuts to eat, and birds he shot and caught with snares, and rabbits and things. And he knew how to plant things good to eat, like corn."

"Then where did he go?" the little boy asked. "Why isn't he here now?"

"He had to go when the white people came. He was afraid of

the white people and they were afraid of him. And because they were afraid they fought each other, and the white man took the Indian's land and made the Indians go away to Oklahoma. They cut down the trees and made farms. They built houses and roads. They built churches and schools. And pretty soon the deer were all gone, and the Indians and the bears and the fish in the streams."

"Then where did the white people go?" he queried. "Why aren't they here?"

"Some of them still are," I said, "but not as many as there used to be. For a long time there were many. All over the mountains they had their little farms. When we go to walk in the mountains you see where the old roads ran that their ox-teams made. You see the places where their houses used to stand and the patches where they cut the trees down and made fields. You can see where they piled up the rocks in the edges of the fields, though big trees grow around the rockpiles now, and where the fields used to be."

"Did they die, too, like the Indians, or go away?"

"Some died and some went away," I said. "It took a long time. What happened came so slowly nobody could quite realize it. With the big trees gone, their leaves didn't fall on the land to make it richer every year. Their roots didn't hold the water on the land. The big rains washed the fields down the sides of the mountains and into the streams and the land grew poorer and poorer, washing away. And the old folks died, and the young folks went away."

"Then what happened?" he wanted to know.

"Then slowly the trees started to come back and cover the fields, and the roads, and the graves of the people who died. And when the trees came back the deer began to come back and the birds and the fish and the little animals."

He was holding the arrowpoint, the Stone Age tool, turning it over in his hand.

"I know what," he said. "Let's write the Indians and tell them to come back again. Tell them we won't hurt them and I will let them shoot my bow and arrow...."

There was a drumming thunder in the sky and the singing birds fell still. A big plane, sunlight glinting on its wings, flew over.

"I'm afraid they've gone too far," I said, "ever to come back again."

Some Thoughts on Bears

Every year in August the members of this inbred little association, which is now going into its third and fourth generation, get
together to transact the small business of the group. We sit out
under trees in the yard of whoever is the chairman that year and
argue such momentous matters as whether or not dogs should be
allowed at the swimming dock. They are always barred, but they
are always there, and we argue whether or not the electric fence
which is supposed to keep the horses from coming and peering in
people's windows is dangerous to small children, and how much it
is going to cost to buy the green stuff which keeps the tennis
courts in shape. Long debates are held as to whether or not we
should drain the lake and somebody always points out that we've
twice drained it and restocked it over the past forty years, and it
didn't seem to make much difference in the fishing.

These matters have been debated so often over the years they
cause no great friction and little comment. A new dog-on-the-
docks committee is formed, a new what-to-do-about-the-flies-the-
horses-cause committee is named, the decision is made to consult
an "authority" on what to do about the lake, and the meeting
adjourns.

This time, though, there was a new item that had not been on

143

the agenda in years past. A bear, it seems, has come down out of the Big Smokies, or somewhere, and has begun to make his nightly rounds of the community garbage cans. So there has arisen a great debate as to what should be done about the bear. Nobody, it seems, wants to do any injury to the bear. Many of the people who have small children would like for the bear to go away, for fear he might do some harm to a child. Others point out that bears are really shy creatures who avoid contact with human beings as much as possible. Others argue that this is only true of well-fed bears.

Hungry bears show no fear of humans at all and will walk right up to picnickers and start eating their sandwiches. For this reason, some of the mothers have decided not to let their children go on picnics or sleep out, as children have been doing here for generations, for fear the bear, smelling food, would come sniffing about as they snooze. In fact, some mothers have even forbidden their children to carry chocolate bars in their pockets when they go to the dock to swim.

There are others, of course, who feel that having a bear in residence adds a little ecological tone to the place, like having a poet or artist in residence adds a cachet of culture to a university, and they think that the bear should be made welcome. If people did not want him raiding their garbage cans at night and scattering papers and empty bottles around—bears are very untidy when they raid garbage cans—he could be frightened away by shining lights on him and blowing whistles, and shouting. He could even be plinked in the backside with a BB. But to keep him in the area, to maintain its wilderness flavor, a pot of honey could be set out in a certain place. The bear would come to this, like deer come to a salt lick, and everybody would be happy, especially the bear.

The Night Was Full
of the Sound of Ballads

Along toward dusk dark the kids tore up what was left of the back porch to use for firewood and got themselves a bunch of marshmallows and some wieners and set out for the lake. The moon rose early, full and glowing, but there was a scud of cloud high up and all you could see was the cold glow of it, casting a pearly radiance over the woods and the lake and the meadows.

And soon, down by the lake, in the luminous night that was neither dark nor bright, you could see the gleam of their fire and in the silence you could hear the sound of singing. So Mama and I eased off down there and sat down in the deep shadows back from the fire so the presence of older folks would not worry them and we listened to them sing.

It was good singing, as any singing is good around a fire at night. They didn't sing the old songs we used to sing, "Carolina Moon," and "Long, Long Trail" and that kind of sentimental song. They sang the old ballads that came across the sea years ago and were nearly forgotten until Burl Ives and some of the lesser folk singers rescued them and made them a part of the world's music again.

There was an Austrian girl there who sang "Lili Marlene" in a voice as sweet and clear as a silver bell. She sang it in German, and, hearing it, I could understand how the soldiers of three armies—the French and the British and the Americans—all adopted the sweet and haunting love song that first was sung by their bitter enemies, the Germans of Rommel's Afrika Corps.

Wars do some good that lasts, for the presence of the Austrian girl here in the Georgia mountains was due to the war. And they spread throughout the world songs of many nations. For around the fire were youngsters who had flown or fought in many lands and they remembered songs they'd heard at the ends of the earth.

There was one that came from England—a simple round, like "Three Blind Mice"—that was a pretty thing. It went, "The Hart he loves the high road, the Hare he loves the hill, the Knight he loves the broad sword, the Lady loves her Will." Nothing much to it but, a beautiful tune and with twenty voices singing it as a round, the sound was wonderful in the moonlit night.

There was another one, too, a street song that beggars sing in Rome, that being translated meant merely this: "I am a pauper, I have nothing, yet I give to you."

They sang until the fire burned low and we left them and went out to slip into the dark lake water, warm as milk from the day's long sun, and the sound of their singing floated over the water, sweet and clear, while the bullfrogs grumped and rumbled and the whippoorwills talked in the dark woods.

Nobody asked me to give my notable rendition of "Waltzing Matilda," which the New Zealanders used to sing down in the islands while they were fighting Japanese. Nor "The Coal Miners' Song," which the Japanese used to sing while they were fighting us. But beyond that little disappointment it was as fine an evening as I've known in a long long time.

Fall Tunes Its Violins

In the evenings you don't notice it, for the side of the mountain that faces me is in shadow and it looks green, green, green,
the dusty, deep, dark green of late summer. But in the morning
it's different, for then the full glow of the morning sun shines on
it and all its colors gleam and glitter. Not much, yet. Just a trace
of yellow here, a glint of crimson there, but enough to tell you
that, though the thermometer may hang around ninety-three
down in the flatlands, up here in the hills the year has already
turned.

Even a blind man would know that the tide of summer had
turned. The wind does not blow with the steady push of a summer wind now, but in little gusts and slackenings. It dances over
the hills, now dying to a whisper, now rising until all the mountainside murmurs and talks with a low, sweet music and the trees
toss their heads in time to this melody. The orchestra of fall is
tuning up.

And there is a thread of cold in the morning wind now, a faint
chill breath that makes a man who has been having his coffee in
the mornings on the porch, in his pajamas, feel a little tingle of
cold at the back of his neck and along his flanks. A woolen shirt
feels good in the mornings now, and at night the kids, who have

been sleeping stripped to the waist and under no covers at all, now curl in their beds like young raccoons in a hollow stump, blankets pulled up to their chins.

In other years, when the deer were here, you would see them often at this time of year. For they come down from the green glades when the leaves begin to turn, and down on the edge of the old golf course you could see them moving in the thickets.

But so far I've seen only two. The other morning, standing out in the yard, I happened to look across the green alders of the creek toward a little meadow on the other side and there she stood, a big doe, nibbling at the grass as unconcernedly as a cow. Her fawn was at her side, still wearing his baby spots, and they didn't see me.

But then the wind must have shifted or something, for all at once she jerked her head up, and in a twinkling of slender legs she was gone, her white flag flashing in the sun. I don't know what signal she gave the little fellow, but as she leaped away he turned and ran too and they disappeared in the woods together.

The other afternoon she was back. I had been watching the meadow for her, and she hadn't come, and then, all of a sudden, she was there and the fawn with her. She strolled about looking and listening, and then put her head down to graze and the people sitting on the porch with me watched her a long time.

The kids were romping and shouting in the back yard and she didn't seem to mind the noise, but when I called them to come and see her and told them to be quiet, they ran through the house and out on the porch and started looking and pointing, and chattering in excited whispers that rose higher and higher.

And maybe the sound of their running feet, or the change in the tone of the voices, or something, alarmed her. For again, all at once, she was gone like a golden arrow.

That was more than a week ago, and she hasn't been seen since, though I've watched for her every day. And I'm afraid she's moved on to some other range and won't be seen again around here. Which is just as well, for somebody would probably shoot her and her fawn, too, if she stuck around.

And I would hate that, for I would like for this place to become a breeding ground, a refuge and safe haven for the deer and all the wild things, bears and raccoons, rabbits and possums, squirrels and turkeys, and all the creatures of the woods that used to be here long ago.

An Expedition Long Dreamed Of

If I live and nothing happens, as folks in my part of the country always used to say when they spoke of their future plans, I will be spending this New Year's Day back up here in the mountains, ten miles from the nearest town. There will be snow on the ground, I hope, and a skim of ice on the lake, and at night it will be so cold that you can hear the tree limbs crack and the sky will be so clear that the evening star will shine with the cold hard beauty of a diamond as it rises over the crest of the mountain across the valley. And I will sit before a good log fire, and doze, and be thankful to the Lord for letting me be here in this place.

For it was not too long ago when I was spending my time in places exotic enough, but not so close to my heart as this. That was when I was moving from one steamy tropic island to another, finding no coolness anywhere, and finding nothing that was cold and hard and clean and sharply outlined, as are the trees of the mountains in winter, but only flamboyant jungle tangled with creepers and bright with languid tropic blooms.

I used to get letters from the mountains that would ruin my happiness for days, though they were meant merely to bring me a breath of home . . . "a deer ran across the road the other morning as we went to the mail box," one said. "Last night we heard a fox barking on a ridge above the house, and the boys saw his tracks where he had crossed the road. . . ." "There was a heavy frost this morning and it looks as if there may be snow. . . ."

I would read these letters as I sat, stripped to shorts, with the sweat pouring off me in some forsaken little hole in the remoter reaches of the Pacific, or as I looked out of a hotel window on the teeming, clamorous street life of Hong Kong. And I swore that when I got home I'd start the New Year where there was only cold and silence, and nobody for miles around.

I know, of course, that this is one well-laid plan that has a good chance of ganging aglae completely, and the chances are that as this sees print I probably will be nursing a set of bruised and splintered hands as I try to blow some life into a fire that won't burn because the wood is wet and a squirrel has made a nest in the chimney. And it probably won't be snowing, but raining, and everything will be clammy and damp and musty, and I will be wishing that I was back on some bright Pacific isle, snoozing in the sun under a palm tree, rousing only now and then to slice the top off a coconut and take a sip of its cool thirst-quenching waters.

In fact, if it has rained, and the back roads around here are like they have been in the past, I probably won't get here at all, even if I park my car and hike in over the frozen roads with a pack on my back. And if I do get here, and it rains, I won't be able to get out for a month. So if these dispatches suddenly cease I'd appreciate it if somebody would break out a team of mules and one of those rock sleds which the mountain folks use and which will go anywhere, and send out a rescue expedition. I'll be waiting as anxiously as a hound pup marooned on a chicken coop in a flood.

Are Panthers Roaming the Hills Again?

One night a few years ago, some of the kids who had been wandering the shores of the lake came in panting and bug-eyed. On the slopes of the old mountain towering above the water, they had heard a wild and eerie sound, a cry like the sound of a woman screaming. Since at that hour of the night all the ladies of the colony were presumably safe and snug at home, with nothing particular to scream about, this report was a great puzzle.

First we tried to argue that maybe what they had heard was a police siren from down the highway. They said it couldn't have been. It came from the side of the mountain directly above where they stood along the road.

Maybe it was an owl, I said. Those old big owls, with tufted ears that poke up like horns, sometimes utter strange cries. Nope, they said, it wasn't an owl. How about a rabbit? A rabbit taken unaware by a weasel, sometimes utters a thin and piercing cry. Nuts, they said. This cry came from no rabbit that ever lived, or died. It was a shriek and a moan and a wail and a sob all at once, they said, and it made the hair stand up on the head, and the flesh to turn cold with goose-bumps.

For several nights thereafter bold spirits wandered the mountain roads, armed with shotguns, listening for the screech to come again. It never did, and gradually the whole thing was forgotten.

Now comes Mr. Herbert Ravenel Sass, the naturalist and author, to cast a ray of light upon the mystery. Writing in the *Saturday Evening Post*, Mr. Sass says that the panther which once roamed the hills and valleys of the Appalachians and the swamps of the Eastern Seaboard, is making a comeback after being, presumably, extinct for years.

He is particularly prevalent in the North Carolina mountains, and since the Georgia hills are an extension of that range, it may be presumed that once in a while a far-roving cat will wander down to Georgia. And, said Mr. Sass, it is the habit of the panther when lonesome, or displeased, to rend the night with a weird and almost human cry.

So what the kids heard, I guess, was an unhappy panther, lonesome for his North Carolina home, to which I hope, by now, he has returned.

From other sources I read that the bobcat is coming back in great numbers in Tennessee, and the coyotes and the armadillos of the Western Plains are being seen farther and farther East. The way the animals are taking over, it wouldn't surprise me if any day now some hinterlander should report that he has found a herd of buffalo out in his pasture munching contentedly.

When the Sun Is High and the Sky is Clear

Down in the flatlands, the heat of summer still lies upon the land. Up here, the first faint chill of autumn has come to put a nip in the air that wasn't there ten days ago. In the hottest summer the days up here are cool and a blanket feels good at night. But this is a different coolness. This is the first faint gnawing of winter's iron teeth, eating up the sun. This is wool-shirt-in-the-morning weather, two-blankets-at-night weather. This is the end of summer.

Already the grassy reaches of the old golf course, grown up now unkept, are beginning to take on the colors of early autumn. Spring's flowers are soft in color and they lie low along the ground. Summer's flowers are few. But the weeds and tall grasses of autumn wave strident banners of gold and crimson and wave them high.

The steep flank of the big mountain over there still wears its deep summer green when the soft clouds darken the sun. But when the sun is high and the sky is clear the colors of autumn begin to show through; the reds and the yellows, the first faint thin traces of brown, bespeak the months to come when all the great green slope will be as bright as flame.

The chill is in the air, but not in the water yet. The energy of summer's suns still are stored in the clear green-yellow lake. But the nip is in the wind and the dozing on the dock is not the joyful dreamy somnolent thing it was. Small fry must be dried off quickly or they turn blue, and only the fat, well-padded elders find comfort in their snoozing.

The mornings are rich with birdsong now, a rare thing to hear, for few birds make their summer residence hereabouts. These are little brown fellows, the vanguard of the fall migrations, pausing to rest on their journey south, and they drive my cat, Galahad, crazy, for they flit about in the blackberry bushes and he leaps for them and there is something distasteful and frustrating to a cat who leaps into a briar bush in pursuit of a bird that has flown.

So dies the summer, the year aging as a man ages, as a watch hand moves, slowly and unseen.

With the coming of the first thin cold, the look of the air changes. The airs of summer, of June and July, are topaz gold. The air of the first cold days has the clear sparkle of a white diamond. The summer airs are heavy with haze. It hides the distant hills. The autumn air is limpid as spring water. Over beyond the lake, the people who live on the high ridge sit on their terrace in the afternoon and count seven ranges of hills, rolling away like billows of the sea, between them and the sunset.

Soon this clear, magnifying air will be gone. The dust of a million pollens will thicken it, turning it yellow gold by day, blue purple at dusk.

Then, with sniffles and thunderous sneezings, the people will leave the lake and the hills, and the chipmunks and the mice will move back into the houses, and the sleet will come, and the snows, and the mountains will sleep again.

Old-Car Buffs

A little plane came murmuring by, its lights no brighter than the light of a winking star, and then it was gone and the sounds of the night suddenly ceased as if all the little creatures were listening. Then around the curve, lights ablaze, skidding on the muddy roads, came an antique Ford and kids climbed out yelling, and dogs yelped and cats scurried, and quiet and peace had ended. But the fun had begun. They were the forerunners of a happy invasion.

There had come a thundering great storm a few hours before that left the dirt road around the lake standing in pools of muddy water in the low places and slick as isinglass on the slopes. And those of us who tried to move around in our heavy, low-slung cars found ourselves fighting the wheel and skidding into the ditches and even when we managed to hold it straight down the middle of the high humpbacked road we'd drag our oilpans with an anguished scraping sound.

Then about eleven o'clock in the morning around the lake there came the most beautiful sight you nearly ever saw. Fifteen antique A-Models in all their classic splendor—phaetons, coupes, sedans, roadsters with rumble seats and ancient wooden-bodied station wagons, every one of them forty years old or older, every one of them as bright of paint and chrome as the day they were new bought, came by in proud processional, their simple four-cylinder engines ticking like watches.

It was a gathering of a special breed of amiable fanatics of whom my son John is one of the looniest!—a group calling itself the Model A Restorers Club, founded nationally in 1952 and now with members in every state. They come from every walk of life. There are lawyers and doctors, teachers and preachers and mechanics and filling station operators and roofers and salesmen, all sharing the same happy obsession. They like to seek out and find old A-models, no matter in what state of disrepair, and fix them up until they look and run like new.

The old cars look a little incongruous on the expressway, tooling along at a serene and stately forty-five while the eighty-mile-an-hour traffic flashes past, but up here in the mountains they are in their element. They were built for these narrow dirt roads and they went over them as nimbly as goats, neither skidding nor sliding nor dragging their bottoms on the gravel. It was almost as if they loved getting back on the roads they were built to travel on.

Some fifteen cars, loaded with old-car buffs, their wives and children sitting proudly beside them, pulled off the highway to eat a picnic lunch before going on over the mountain to chug stoutly up the steep road to Amicalola Falls. For they hold to the theory that there is nowhere an old A-Model cannot go. And they may be right, for if they can make that climb to the falls overlook, without having to get out and push, there *is* nowhere they cannot go.

P.S. They made it.

Animal Kingdom Is Busy at Its Chores

It is the time of evening now when all the birds are singing their farewell to the dying day—the time that has a magic in it, when the winds are still and no leaf stirs and all the valley is filled with birdsong and the low, deep, steady humming of a million bees. It is a good time to be alone, to sit and look and listen to try to understand the miracle of the sunset hour, when one last great blaze of golden light falls on the earth and all is still and clearly seen for a moment before the shadows rise and darkness comes.

A moment ago a humming bird, a little fellow no bigger than the first joint of my thumb, came on roaring wings into the shadow of the porch two feet away from my head. He stood upright on empty air, his wings ablur, peering with a tiny black eye at the vase of wild flowers on the table. He hung there for ten seconds probably, a little graybreasted fellow in a bright blue long-tailed coat, then he saw me and moved over and hung for a moment before my face, his slim bill poised like a dagger a foot away from my nose. Then in motion so fast the eye could not follow him he was gone.

From the back porch comes a muffled thumping sound where the dog burrows deep into the earth, furiously digging to no avail for the old groundhog who for years made his residence there.

He would be living there still, unmolested, if his curiosity hadn't gotten the best of him. Anxious to know what was going on up above, he gnawed a hole in the corner of the porch, where the winter rains had softened the boards. From here when there was traffic on the porch, he would peer inquisitively, whiskers twitching.

A groundhog seen from a distance is one thing. A groundhog seen fixing you with a beady eye from three paces is something else again. So now the porch is gone, ripped up to reveal a maze of tunnels and burrows going deep into the earth. And all I've seen of the dog for three days is his back end as he disappears into these tunnels. There from morn to night he digs furiously with growls and sniffs and snortings, casting earth behind him in a spray.

Tomorrow his happy days of digging will be ended and so I trust will be the groundhog's residence beneath my roof. The man comes to pour a new floor, of concrete this time, guaranteed to be rain and groundhog proof. But I'll miss the old fellow and so I guess will the dog.

The groundhog is sealed off with maledictions. New arrivals are welcomed with glad cries. From the window back of where I sit comes the faint mewing of three new-born kittens, little groping fellows with tiger-like square heads and gray tails. They are still blind and helpless.

As calmly as if such a thing happened to her every day, the slim gray cat, their mother, washed and dried them and set them to their lunch.

So life goes on—the birds singing, the kittens mewing, the bees at work, the dog digging furiously for his prey slumbering deep in the earth, as the day ends and night comes to the mountain.

A Mountain Murmurs
Its Ancient Wisdom

I sneaked off up to the mountains the other day, feeling a little guilty to be taking a vacation in this quiet spot while far off in Korea men were getting killed in hills and valleys that are bright with autumn now, but where there is no quietness and no peace.

I felt sort of ashamed of myself for being there, just doing nothing for three days but walking the hills in the clear gold of the sunshine, sitting in the evening watching the big stars rise, and at night, lying on the floor in front of a fire where oak logs steamed and crackled and filled the room with warmth and that fine good smell that somehow always takes me back to my boyhood, and the old days when such a fire as this burned on my grandfather's hearth.

It didn't take long for the magic of the hills to begin its work, though, and soon I somehow didn't mind being there, doing nothing but resting and sitting and watching the day come in a pearly shimmer beyond the hills, watching birds flying in the bright blue afternoons, when in the clear air the hillsides flamed and burned like molten gold, watching the long, slow dying of the sun and the coming of the dark, when far off down the valley the lake was first silver and then the blue steel of the gun barrel and then a glint of crimson in the last light, and then only a darker shadow in the deep shadow of the hills.

I don't know which was the best time, the crisp, cool, clean, quiet mornings, or the sleepy afternoons, or the long twilights, or the starbright evenings when there was no sound, not even the call of owl or whippoorwill, and the world was as quiet as if there was no life in all the land.

And all day it was still. Then, far in the night, lying there half waking and half sleeping while the dying fire cast its last flickering highlights on the old wooden walls, I could hear the little wind begin to blow. First it was only a whisper in the leaves of the oak outside the window, and then a murmur and a rustle, and then it whimpered and moaned a little, and in it was all loneliness and all longing, and all the vague regrets a man feels in his heart sometimes when in darkness and quietness he reads his own soul and listens to the gentle rebuke of his conscience for things undone that should have been done, and things done that should not have been done.

And across the wide meadow, where the little field mice make their tunnels in the grass, where the fox prowls and the possum walks, hunting the ripening persimmons, where the deer comes to graze on moonlight nights, his proud head lifting to scent the wind, the old dark mountain began to whisper in its sleep.

All along the great face of the hill the wind walked the treetops and the voice of the mountain was the voice of a million million of leaves and the murmuring voice of the mountain was a soothing sound. It seemed to say that a man walks a little while upon this earth and that he goes down strange roads and sees many fearful and wondrous things, and he cannot expect all roads he walks to be smooth, nor all his days to be bright.

And with the old mountain murmuring its ancient wisdom and the firelight glowing and the good smell of woodsmoke in the room I went to sleep. And it was a good three days, as good as ever I spent I guess, and as good as ever I'll see again.

A Fine Way to End

It was a fine way to end the summer, sitting on the porch in an old-fashioned rocking chair, looking out across the meadow, aglow with wildflowers, to the steep flanks of old Burnt Mountain, just beginning to change its dress from summer's dusty green to the gold and crimson of the coming fall.

It was a peaceful and restoring moment, doing much to ease the shock of seeing the lake no longer a shimmer of blue water but a deep raw wound in the earth. We do this about every ten or fifteen years, so that the trash fish can be seined out and the lake restocked. But it is always a strange feeling to see the land, no smooth bowl but a crater marked with many deeps and shallows, the bare ribs of the ancient earth showing through. The stumps still stand where the forests were, and the open places that were the old cornfields, and the deep gullies cut by the wheels of the pioneer wagons can still be seen.

So it was good sitting there in the dusk, out of sight of the lake, watching the dark come on, and listening to the crickets tune their fiddle strings, and the little peepers, the tree frogs, I guess they were, hitting a few tentative practice notes on their flutes. And down the valley to the west a cloud the shape of a golden seashell faded, leaving nothing on the earth but a soft blue haze.

And now with the coming of the deep dark the full orchestra of the night began to play, crickets and tree frogs in one pulsing harmony. And now the stars began to wink and twinkle, high and far, except one bright one, Venus, maybe, that rose just above the brooding black hulk of the mountain, and hung there, so close it looked as if you could reach out and take it in your hand.

And I guess that no matter where I may wander, to faraway places with strange sounding names, to live for awhile among people speaking languages I don't understand, I will always remember this place, and this night, and the people I've known and loved here in these hills.

And I will always want to come back to them.

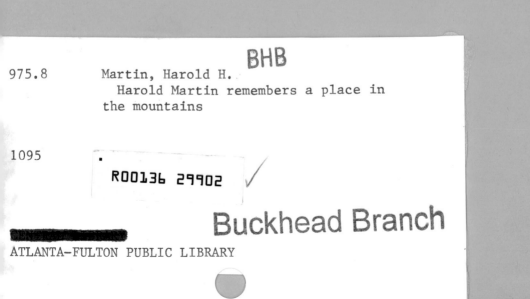